Production Focus:
Theories, Strategies, and Developing a Structure

Baisham Chatterjee

iUniverse, Inc.
Bloomington

Production focus: Theories, strategies, and developing a structure

Copyright © 2012 by Baisham Chatterjee.

All rights reserved. No part of this book may be used or reproduced by any means, graphic, electronic, or mechanical, including photocopying, recording, taping or by any information storage retrieval system without the written permission of the publisher except in the case of brief quotations embodied in critical articles and reviews.

iUniverse books may be ordered through booksellers or by contacting:

iUniverse
1663 Liberty Drive
Bloomington, IN 47403
www.iuniverse.com
1-800-Authors (1-800-288-4677)

Because of the dynamic nature of the Internet, any web addresses or links contained in this book may have changed since publication and may no longer be valid. The views expressed in this work are solely those of the author and do not necessarily reflect the views of the publisher, and the publisher hereby disclaims any responsibility for them.

Any people depicted in stock imagery provided by Thinkstock are models, and such images are being used for illustrative purposes only.
Certain stock imagery © Thinkstock.

ISBN: 978-1-4759-1718-5 (sc)

Printed in the United States of America

iUniverse rev. date: 4/30/2012

Contents

Acknowledgements vii
Author Biography ix
Preface & Introduction xi

Chapter 1	Product design and product strategy 1	
Chapter 2	New product generation techniques through reengineering 24	
Chapter 3	Manufacturing strategy and revolutionizing product development 41	
Chapter 4	Production analysis, synthesis and project management 60	
Chapter 5	Production focus and processes for development, the ideal economics, How it started? 78	
Chapter 6	A more advanced form of process management and industrial management 95	
Chapter 7	Construction management 118	
Chapter 8	Essentials of total quality management and beyond it 138	
Chapter 9	Total quality control and plant performance 158	

Conclusion 185
Reference 195

Acknowledgements

I would like to thank Manik Mondal of the NIT Durgapur library for all the data that I received from him. I also thank PropelICT in Saint John for the project that made me successful. I would also like to thank Stephen Bernhut (Ivey business journal), Gerry Pond (Mariner Partners), Mark Hollingworth (McGill university), Martijn J Fransen (PANalytical), Daniel Doiron (UNB), Gerhard Schreck(Pamas Gmbh), Partha Dasgupta (Cambridge university), Avijit Vinayak Banerjee (MIT), Kunal Basu (Oxford university), Dilip Mookherjee (Boston university), Rahul N Mazumdar (Rahul Foundation), Neelotpaul Banerjee (NIT Durgapur). I also thank my little brother Ganesh who died thousands of years ago but he fills my heart and soul when I listen to him talking.

Author Biography

The author has published 3 very creative books with iUniverse, among them Finding the innovation gap: Disruptive idea, a better way of managing prototypes and Organization Development: Developing the processes and resources for high-tech businesses being the most interesting and extensive piece of work. The author also has 37 research findings at Ivey business Journals and has completed many projects on organization development, e-commerce, economics and strategy and has been a very creative blogger and communicating the creativity and future of North America, the US and Europe through various blogging sites and the most extensive of his projects being that of PANalytical and the most creative being that of Propel ICT.

Preface & Introduction

In this introductory part the part and sub-part of all the chapters have been described.

In Chapter 1 on product design and product strategy the product design stage has been discussed including the product development processes, product typology, development decisions, assembly process. Other factors discussed are s-curve, (ABS)-Antilock Brake System, SOPs, SOAV (slide out auxiliary visor), product portfolio architecture, product cost assumption, different ways to reduce engineering conflicts, embodiment design, three stages of the natural energy, design for manufacture, product matrix, material selection, physical prototype construction, design of experiments, CSV(core strategic vision), E-commerce and pricing strategy and platform lifecycles.

In Chapter 2 on new product generation techniques through reengineering the talked about components are Product planning, product lines, product safety, product development, product proliferation, Product testing, PLM, PLM software suites, PLM applications, design cycle, traceability, theory of productivity, lean manufacturing, IT Value Map, capturing and categorizing exemplars of practice, mock ups and prototypes, ECOs or engineering change orders, organizational reengineering and manufacturing pipelines.

In Chapter 3 on manufacturing strategy and revolutionizing product development the sub-components are, the task of a company's manufacturing function, automation, manufacturing capability and manufacturing operations, mass customization, organic organization, trade-offs, assignment of modern design engineers, MRP, continuous flows, materials planning methods, mass production, 4th generation language (4GL), DRP (distribution resource planning), MEI, R&D group functions, MEI 2010 which is composed of design, marketing and testing, evaluate quality, QFD, and DFM, product building capability, and the purpose of prototyping.

In Chapter 4 on production analysis, synthesis and project management the sub-components are conversion facilities, chain reaction, product organization, distribution method, where R&D fits, CPM (critical path method), aggregate planning models, facilities layout, plant layout, adjustable equipment, machine tooling, production control designs, product designers, order control, production stage, product designers system, production-improvement effort, productivity per phase, non-fabricating systems, applying the fundamental theory of linear programming, flow charts, purchase of fabricated units of components, and site acquisitions activity.

In Chapter 5 the sub-components are the relationship between information and control systems, continuous models, breakeven points, equipment costs, plant capacity, production processes, equipment costs, layouts and models, PERT and CPM, standard types of conveying equipment, layouts and models, production standards, sub-optimization, quantity control, Gantt chart, constructing a schedule for an assembled product, cost control, maintenance, cost data and cost improvement programs.

In chapter 6 on a more advanced form of process management and industrial management the sub-components are process determination, technological evaluation, production equipment selection criteria, a few ways of making process technology changes, EPA or environment protection agency, product improvement, evaluating processes and investment, production management cost control, capacity and economic life of machines, PERT and CPM, product design and process layout, Hawthorne effect, planning and pre-production, optimal design of tools and equipment control, inventory turnover and labor skills, ordering costs, inventory policy and inventory models, materials requirement planning, inspection procedures in production, sequence of processing steps, production controls responsibility, approaches to maintaining equipment, technology change, frequency of maintenance, technology change, confidential information.

In chapter 7 on construction management various types of construction work has been described, purchasing and equipment management function, submitting proposal for a given project, contractors creativity, cash budget, construction law, preventive maintenance, machine system performance, control records, construction market, construction methods, construction projects, construction operations, project duration, effective cost control, data processing systems and techniques, cost keeping for construction equipment, inflationary cycle all have been discussed in detail.

In chapter 8 on essentials of total quality management and beyond it the descriptions are on TQM formulations and applications, zero defects, strategy formulation, quality goals, company-wide quality control, operational tasks, standardization means, Quality function deployment, qualitative information, statistical control limits, demand in equipment, variations in equipment, fluctuations in demand, continuous quality improvement and examples of St Mary's and Toyota have been taken, moreover further descriptions have been made on permanent process improvement, QMS, quality costs, WIP, DFMA(design for manufacture and assembly), FMEA(failure mode and effect analysis), total productive maintenance and statistical process control (SPC).

In chapter 9 on total quality control and plant performance descriptions have been made on MIL-Q-9858 or its derivative standards, final design models, design contract calls, operational requirements, value engineering, relative reliabilities of the later generation systems, normal technological evolution, sourcing quality control, design limits, quality control plan, design changes, CRMs, quality audit, calibration audit, points of control, quality control techniques, quality information equipment subsystem, control gaging, acceptance sampling procedures such as MIL-STD-105 A, product strength and environmental stress value, availability performance, quality product goal, availability engineering, availability models, materials engineering and maintenance, and strategic cycle.

Chapter 1

Product design and product strategy
(By Baisham Chatterjee)

Product development processes has three stages: understand the opportunity, develop a concept and implement a concept. A product development phase can be thought of as a sequence of parallel and serial activities or steps to be completed. Within each phase there are concurrent development activities that occur. Mechanical design proceeds in parallel to electrical design in parallel with software code development. Many companies force the periodic assembling of the product as it stands at a given point of time, along with its associated forecasted systems that remain uncertain. The assembly process is executed to obtain, a better picture of the design as it is evolving, to evaluate that preliminary system to freeze parts of the design. Some development decisions are made final like general layout, user operation, control, suppliers. The development process is known as stage-gate process or waterfall development process where there are stages or phases or activities in the development work followed by periodic gates. A gate is an evaluation by the upper management or team stage so that the product can be carried to the next stage. Product development phase looks at product launch and at the end of the product definition phase they ensure there is market for the product. Similar to product designing there are three product redesigning strategies. The product typology can be maintained and parametric redesign explored-changes in thickness or geometry of components or changes in materials. They can be placed in different topologies of the functional model and can be replaced by functional layout or with different core technologies. Unbiased prediction, customer-driven design, analysis using basic principles, and hands-on experimentation are the philosophy underpinnings of redesign methodology. It may be appropriate to perform adaptive or original changes before creating and optimizing a design model.

There are many design theories using new technology that becomes more complex. The explosive growth of computing ability has tremendous impact on engineering design. There is a complex, static and dynamic analysis of product design before gate decisions are made. There are parametric values and demand for rapid development that is pushing for algorithmic synthesis of mechanical solutions. Product development processes and the task breakdown among team members should enhance and encourage the imagination and effectiveness of the human participants. These processes and their organization should not erect hurdles or roadblocks that must be leaped or bypassed, but must assist in stimulating our natural creativity. As products historically become more complex and users more diverse, a gradual dichotomy between design and manufacturing was inevitable. Product development requires collective knowledge generation and control documentation describes the new product.

Technological innovations typically manifest themselves into a market along an s-curve timeline behavior. In the s-curve at first the values are low and widely spaced: not much innovation is occurring in the market, since its difficult to introduce. Next, a rapid profusion of innovation occurs, and many products are typically launched in time, by those who join the market. Innovators typically conceive of a even newer technology that can provide even better performance. This technology is introduced for the first time into the market and then develops its own s-curve behavior. The new s-curve is a disruptive technology that requires changes in the market system for the product to succeed. The improved performance of technology is sufficient to force these changes. The development of fluorescent lamps required new fixtures and ballast technology and incandescent bulbs did not require. Moreover looking at the other factors there is a spectrum of customer satisfaction from disgust to delight that changes the increased implementation of function. The more product function implemented, the more the customer expects and the harder it becomes to delight the customer. Further the harder it is to supply expected basic performance. When antilock brake system emerged in the market (ABS), they represented a significant step over linear quality. As ABS reduces cost, it is placed on a wider array of automobile types and classes representing linear quality of those models.

To help reconstruct everything there is something known as the functional modeling. At first the process has to be specified by which the product would be lastly designed. A process description in the sense includes: preparation, execution and conclusion. Within each phase the high level user activities are networked to show the full life-cycle of a product from purchase to recycling or disposal. To focus on product usage, the system boundary chosen includes all the customer activities such as purchasing, transporting, clipping, storage and picking. The structure to understand a power screwdrivers different qualities depend upon functional mapping that has a number of implications. These implications include: parallel and sequential function chains, denoting possible assemblies sub-assemblies and modules; high-level physical models of the transform of information, energies and signals; consistency of flow transformation from function to function, boundary conditions based on the entering flows and so forth.

Through the additional information and logic, function structures, have a number of advantages over a simpler function-tree approach. These advantages have clear benefits as a product reaches later stages of development. Function structures, based on task listing, have a clear and explicit relationship to customer needs. Since flows are not represented, customer needs are not tied directly to any sequence of functions. Function structure illustrates parallel and sequential functional relationship, by default. Such relationships are critical for making product architecture decisions early in the development cycle. They lead to assemblies, sub-assemblies and tem resource allocation including module interface issues. Ultimately a set of virtual analysis of physical prototypes will be constructed for any product. To develop such prototypes high-level models are needed of the product performance. Function structures provide one source of this information in terms of materials, energies and signals.

Product teardown helps us to understand the engineering manifested within a current product. It also exposes creative avenues for product evolution. The first an automobile auxiliary visor subsystem, focuses on the tools for teardown like SOPs and force flow diagrams. A slide-out auxiliary visor (SOAV) as a part of the complete overhead ceiling unit. This visor is supplied to a luxury automobile manufacturer. It blocks light in the front range of the driver or passenger and shields light from the side. Looking at the SOAV redesign it helps in disassembling the SOAV, the strategy is to use 2 products. It acts as a reference as the other one is disassembled. Each part is disassembled at a time, once it is completely disassembled it is reassembled using the aid of Disassembly process table.

Competitive benchmarking is a very vital process used over here and before it is brushed off one should realize that very few market leaders consistently produce the leading technology in the market. There is always a potential for some unknown competitor to have great idea that can change the market. Markets generally have stable planned behavior and never do in the long term. Further in establishing a roadmap, it is often necessary to benchmark technology from industries outside of ones immediate market. Just because a competitor uses a new product technology does not necessarily mean that ones company should do so as well. It does mean one should develop a competitive strategy that would attack the market. Doing so will mean that a company always develops products that would lag the competition. Also the competition may be taking a gamble on a new technology that may not be accepted. Having benchmarked competitive products on customer and technical criteria, the next step is to use this information to set targets for a new product development effort. Since new product specifications are the purpose behind and culmination of the benchmarking process, the benchmarking process describes potential openings in the market and so establish what it would take to take advantage of those opportunities. Specifications for a new product are quantitative, measurable criteria and the product should be designed to satisfy. They are the measurable goals for the design team. Design information should be established early and revisited often. Functional requirements are statements of the specific performance of a design that is what the device should do. Functional relationships should focus on performance, be stated in terms of logical relationships and are stated initially in solution neutral terms. Constraints are external factors that might limit the selection of system or sub-system characteristics. They generally apply to the set of functions for the system. Cost and schedule, size, weight, materials properties and safety issues such as nontoxic, nonflammable materials are constraints. Specifications relative to surface finish and tolerances may or may not be considered constraints. In the specifications case in the specification sheet template the functional requirements and constraints are logically consistent. It is important to know that the customer needs and the specifications are to be met and they are technologically and economically feasible. The customer should be made aware if a system cannot be built to meet the stated specifications.

It is important to quantify wherever possible. The team may begin with rather qualitative statements, but it is important in the end, to develop a quantitative statement of the specification. It is important to determine detailed approaches for ultimately testing and verifying the specifications during the product development process. Examples are engineering analysis; tests of scale, full size or partial or complete prototypes; checks of engineering drawings; failure mode analysis or user tests with the appropriate sample size.

A product portfolio architecture is the system strategy for laying out components and systems on multiple products to best satisfy future and current market needs. There are two basic corporate objectives considered in developing a product portfolio architecture: costs and revenue. Revenues increase with expanded offerings in a large portfolio, as a company can then make products more tailored to each customer in the market. Costs go up in developing, supporting, and manufacturing a larger set of different products. Thus the decisions made about how to support multiple products can have a large impact on the overall profitability of a product portfolio. Choosing a portfolio with a large number of unique products has the potential for high revenue from multiple market segments but incurs a high production cost due to the manufacturing complexity. A single product has low production cost but also has low marketing satisfaction. To explore portfolio design, portfolio architectures have to be explored. Labeling creates classification and we use market demands as the basis of dividing portfolio architectures. Portfolio architecture falls into three basic categories: fixed un-sharing, platform and massively customizable. Fixed un-sharing architecture is typically applied when the product has very high volumes, implying that economies of scale exist to remain competitive. Magnetic storage media is one such example. Manufacturers do not really care if their VHS tape can share components with their cassette tape; each must be minimal in cost. This choice typically means application of design for assembly principles to the product to reduce the number of parts. This application of assembly principles consequently increases the function sharing of each part, implemented using complex injection molded practices. A complex part is less likely to be reused on a different product in the portfolio. Fixed un-sharing architecture can be further classified into two types, those of a single level of performance and those of a robust nature. That is a market that may seek variety. The fixed offering may provide only one option to the entire market and be less than ideal for many customers. When a company offers products that share components, modules, or systems to meet market variety, we call the configuration layout, within the set of products and their shared elements, a platform portfolio architecture. The common components modules and systems are also called the platform, and the supported products are called the variants. There are at least four types of platform architectures: modular product families, modular product generations, consumable platform architecture, and adjustable-for purchase architecture. One consequential opportunity of a modular platform architecture is the development of derivative products. These are family variants that arise historically by taking an original product and making changes to it to offer more products. Because of the established product design of the original product, the development of derivative products requires less cycle time and project costs. A part of it is the cost-reduced derivative i.e the cost of an original product in a family is reduced by choosing alternative materials, removing product features, improving production efficiency or optimizing aspects that were originally overdesigned. The new product is offered separately in the product family, and the majority of the cost savings in passed on to the customer. The second part is the product line extensions where the features are extended or modified to address more customer needs or a different market or sub-market. Alternatively the current design features of a product are redesigned to improve engineering metrics, such as accuracy, reliability and durability. This type of derivative product is only an extension of the original product, without significant price increases passed on to the customer. Enhanced products are the third type that forms from a basic model adding additional features that address alternative markets or more difficult customer needs. The original product features however are redesigned and extended into a platform where the platform interfaces are planned to support multiple variants.

    Production cost assumption starts by creating a product architecture that divides along a company's existing organization structure or its extended enterprise. Ex-it may be that a company outsources the design of all electronic controls for a product. This might make sense to divide the portfolio architecture isolating the electronics on all products making electronic controls form a modular family platform. The underlying market dynamics that give rise to different portfolio architecture are the interaction between different market variety from different customers. Some architectures are more adaptable for a design team to meet the variety of different customers; other architectures are more responsive to a customer who wants to use the product under different circumstances.

There can be many different ways introduced to reduce engineering conflicts in the modern world which are by dividing the object into independent parts that are easy to disassemble and increase the degree of segmentation as much as possible. Either the disturbing part or the necessary part should be removed from the object. It is important to change the environment from homogeneous to non-homogeneous and look that different parts of the object carry different functions. There are around 40 operations and the next says that it is important to merge homogenous objects or those intended for contiguous operations. Attach an aerodynamic lift to the object, compensate for the low reliability of an object and introduce protections before the action is performed. Increase the objects degree of freedom and use a multi-layered assembly line instead of a single layer. Incline the object or turn it at its side. Make the object vibrate and increase the frequency of vibration like resonance, piezo vibration, ultrasonic or electromagnetic vibration. Used pulsed actions with pauses between impulses. The object should service and repair itself and waste products from the objects should be used to produce the desired action. Instead of unavailable, complicated or fragile objects, a simplified cheap copy can be used. The object can be replaced by an optical copy and make use of scale effects. An expensive objects that have longer life can be replaced with many cheaper objects with shorter life. Use colored additives to observe certain objects or processes. Use materials with different thermal expansion coefficients. Use composites instead of homogeneous materials.

As a purpose of many embodiment design methods in the product life cycle there are methods that range from mathematical and empirical modeling of a product's performance to the life cycle issues of service and environment impact. Modeling methods provide us with a means of representing the performance and potential failure states of a product across its customer needs and engineering specifications. Design for manufacturing and assembly techniques provide a systematic approach for ensuring the producibility, availability and economics of a product venture. Physical prototyping methods then provide a process for testing for actual performance and manufacturability of a product. When studying the product development process it is important to understand the intrinsic complexity and non-linearity of the process. There are three stages of the natural energy bilge pump product, where the first stage includes customer needs analysis, functional modeling and product architectural layout. At this stage, the physical embodiment of the product is very fuzzy. The product is understood as an input output system that converts energy from the environment to water flow from a pleasure craft. The business case opportunity and engineering specifications are investigated and documented. However, an actual physical concept has not been created in any concrete or tangible vision. In the next stage of the process concepts are developed as line drawings and high-level geometric descriptions. The focus is on the operational principles of the product. Detailed geometry, shape, material are unknown. The concept embodiment stage seeks to resolve the focus of the product to a singular crisp description. This involves thousands and thousands of decisions and design parameter choices depending on the scale of the product. Embodiment design applies to when the whole product architecture is developed from scratch.

Before a product model is considered, a product development team must take stock of its current design status. A wealth of data usually exists when analytical models are being developed for product concepts. These data include organized customer needs list, activity diagram, business cases, functional models, engineering specifications within a house of quality, teardown data of past and or competitive products, s-curve trend analysis for forecasted improvements, product architecture layout and chosen product concepts. Not all aspects of a product may be modeled mathematically. Practical limitations exist in the complexity of the model. It may require excessive computational resources or take too much time to develop accurately, and there will be limitations of the model in predicting performance. The performance metrics to understand the design variables and how much safety margin can be predicted: The predicted model accuracy over the entire development process, includes the prototyping stage versus modeling cost in terms of the resources. Detailed models helps in understanding the design concept as unlikely as through prototyping. Producing better results depends on the difficulty of the prototype construction and experimentation process. An experimental prototype can help experimentally construct a first-order statistical model of the performance metric in terms of the design variable through structured variations of the prototype. There must be a one to one correspondence between a performance metric and an informal objective. By knowing the value of the performance metric the associated objective is achieved at a target value. At the end of the modeling process, knowing a performance metric value will allow an informal interpretation of the achievement level of the associated objective.

Design for manufacture (DFM) entails making piece parts easier to produce from raw stock. One can make a plastic part easier to injection mold by changing the draft angle-the angle formed by the difference in wall thickness from the part at the inside of the mold considered with the wall thickness at the end of the mold. Design for manufacture involves application of part-forming models, whether they are basic rules, analytic formulas, or complex final element process simulations. Design for assembly entails making attachment directions and methods simpler, for making a part easy to attach by using snap fits instead of machine screws. It involves attachment of application times and complexity models, whether they are basic rules, tables based on simplified time studies or full-time and motion industrial engineering studies. Design for manufacture and assembly has three beneficial impacts. It reduces part count thereby reducing cost. Similarly the product structure guidelines shows that the designing of a product should be done so that it is multifunctional with more eco-efficient than many unique function products. Minimize the number of parts and create multi-functional parts reducing disassembly time and resources. It is important to avoid separate springs, pulleys or harnesses and instead embed these functions into parts to reduce disassembly time and resources. It is important to make designs as modular as possible with a separation of functions that allows options of service, upgrade or recycling along with designing a reusable platform with reusable modules. Locate unrecyclable parts in one subsystem that can be quickly removed and helps speed disassembly. Locate parts with the highest value in easily accessible places with an optimized removal direction because it enables partial disassembly for optimal return. Design parts are used for stability during disassembly and manual disassembly is faster with a firm working base. In the structuring process in plastic parts, they may avoid embedded metal inserts or reinforcements that creates the need for shredding and separation. Access and break points should be made obvious so that logical structure spreads disassembly and training. It is important to specify manufactured parts to stimulate demand for manufacturing, and reducing raw material consumption. Specifying reusable containers for shipping or consumables within the product reduces raw material consumption. Designing power-down features for different subsystems in a product when they are not in use because it eliminates unnecessary power consumption for idle components.

Material selection guidelines also lead to developing the design for the environment. If regulated materials are avoided and restricted, they are of high impact. It is important to minimize the number of different types of material that simplifies the recycling process. For attached parts, standardize on the same or a compatible material and eliminate incompatible materials that reduces the need for disassembly and sorting. Mark the material on all parts and use recycled materials that would increase the value of the materials and stimulate the market for the material that has been recycled. Use high strength to weight materials on moving parts and use low alloy metals that are more recyclable than high alloy ones that leads to reducing moving mass and therefore energy consumption and more pure metals can be recycled into more varied applications.

In the product matrix that consists of resource extraction, product manufacture and consists of amounts like materials choice, energy use, solid residues, liquid residues and gaseous residues where material choice and energy use are rated low because in the difficulty in extracting copper. Residues are assumed to be present but relatively minimized during the extraction phase for all of the materials. To complete the matrix, knowledge of recycling efforts must be understood. Metals and plastic should be either stamped or recycled. The additional injection molded plastic pieces will always have scrap available for recycling. The packaging and transport of the product have relatively little impact on the overall environmental impact of the product. The choice of foam as a portion of the packaging is questionable because folded cardboard could also be used in place of the more environmentally damaging foam. Very elaborate printing is used over the package. Energy use during transport and packaging appears to be kept to a minimum. The modeling of product metrics is validated into the optimization statement: the selection of a set of variables to describe the design concept. The identification of the noise variables that will affect the robustness of the modeling result. The selection of the objective function from the model, expressed in terms of the design and noise variables, that we seek to minimize or maximize. A feasible design has to be prepared that satisfies the product metrics to the best degree. A basic method to explore and solve product models is what we call a spreadsheet search. Spreadsheets are powerful analysis and data representation tools. They offer a simple means to study a range of product scenarios resulting from the variations of a number of variables. Spreadsheet programs originated out of the need for tools to perform accounting and finance analysis. With personal computers on desks in industry and in the home, all types of professionals now use spreadsheets. Engineers need it the most. It is important to solve a model to determine preferred design variable values and gain insight into the physics and sensitivity on how a product will perform. Design variables are input through design queries. Adjustments are inputs to the product model representing product responses to the end users queries. Spreadsheets can satisfy these model solution goals at least at a basic level, through two steps: planning and design of a product model worksheet and developing and executing a solution procedure. The first step of a product model worksheet is to identify the purpose of the work sheet. The nest step is to determine the outputs that are desired from worksheet analysis. The outputs for product development are the metric values that represent the customer needs determined through product modeling. Once a strategy is chosen, a worksheet layout must be developed. This development entails the arrangement of the input, calculation, output and summary blocks for the worksheet. Many spreadsheet programs provide different color palettes, fonts, border, shading, etc to aid in the worksheet layout. The optimization method presented in the chapter only determine a minimum over a restricted set. No guarantee is provided to determine a global optimum when there may exist a local optima. Methods such as simulated annealing take a problematic approach, genetic algorithms apply domain split heuristics and searching heuristics. It cannot be guaranteed that a global optimum will be found with a numerical search, since it is probably an exhaustively hard problem. Multiple starting points can be used into the space until the global optima based on the local optima can be uncovered.

Many reasons exist for the realistic shortfall of analytical models, including accuracy, development time and model intent. The accuracy of such models due to theoretical limitations may poorly estimate the actual product behavior. If the underlying physics of a product is not well understood, analytical estimates cannot be expected to produce accurate results. A detailed numerical model may need months of development. The efficacy of physical models is pronounced for this situation. Finally an extreme case of incomplete analytical modeling relates to the intent of the prototype. This intent may be to satisfy a milestone or demonstrate ergonomic effects that do not have analytical representations. Physical prototype construction and analysis will continue to be a critical aspect of product realization. Thus on one hand product development demands the effective use of prototypes throughout the development cycle. Paper and virtual models hide the mysteries on how a product would perform. It is not practical to build a large number of physical prototypes at every miniscule step of a products creation. Product development drivers inhibit the fabrication of even a fraction of the prototypes that would be needed. Physical models were at the initial stage of the product understanding constructed whether or not clear answers were given to the prototype tests. The solution to the conflict of physical prototypes lies in technological developments. Computational modeling can become more complex, but at less expense in time due to advances in software tools and hardware performance. It is also becoming faster. Stereo lithography, selective laser sintering, and other rapid prototyping technologies permit physical prototyping with limited impact on schedule. Many product development teams are evaluating and adjusting the balance between virtual and physical analysis with the recent advances in prototyping process. Modern teams that develop on the physical prototypes can exploit recent advances to both reduce time-to-market and positively impact product quality. The different types of prototypes can be described as: The first part i.e the proof of concept models are used to answer specific questions of feasibility about a product. They are usually fabricated from simple, readily available material, where they focus on components and subsystems of the product, and they are constructed post-concept generation usually during concept selection and product embodiment. Industrial design prototypes demonstrate the look and feel of the product. They are initially constructed out of simple material such as foam and foam core and seek to demonstrate many options quickly. A mock up made up of plastic components provides the best solution. Design of experiments (DOE) experimental prototypes are focused physical models where empirical data is sought to parameterize, lay out or shape aspects of the product. The focus with DOE prototypes is usually to model a subsystem of a product while converging to a target performance of the subsystem. Prototypes are fabricated from similar materials and geometry as the actual product, with the DOE prototype being just similar enough to replicate the real products physics, but otherwise made as simply, cheaply and as quickly as possible. Regarding overall layout alpha prototypes are constructed. Alpha prototypes are fabricated regarding materials, geometry, and the layout that the design team believes will be used for the actual product. The alpha is the first system construction of the subsystems that are individually proven in the subsystem DOE prototyping or design. Alphas also usually include some functional features for testing and measurement of the product as a system. They contain limited numbers of the parts manufactured as in final product, through original equipment manufacturers components and exact. Beta prototypes on the other hand are the full-scale functional prototypes of a product, constructed from the actual materials as the final product. They may not necessarily be fabricated using the same production processes as the final product though. Plastic parts on beta prototype are typically CNC machined rather than individually injection molded. Test plans are applied to the functional beta prototype over a range of product functions and operating conditions. Preproduction prototypes are the final class of physical models. These prototypes are used to perform a final part production and assembly assessment using the actual production tooling. Many design firms strive to make the beta prototype be both the preproduction unit and the actual unit; that is to have no corrections needed in the beta prototype.

In the commercial rapid prototyping processes and in their product development processes, it is important to have proficient concepts of them. This process has helped accelerate development cycle times and productivity. Prototypes lead to visualizing concepts as physical entity, market research for ergonomic use and aesthetics, prototypes for functional testing, assembly and manufacturing feasibility, molds for castings, verification of design changes, cost analysis and early marketing promotions. Laser fusion processes use lasers to fuse powder layers, creating the final part cross-section in each layer. A well known process is selective laser sintering. It starts with a thin evenly distributed layer of powder. A laser is then used to sinter the powder in a cross-section, the energy added by the laser heats the powder into a melted state and individual particles coalesce into a solid. Once the laser has scanned the entire cross-section another layer of powder is spread on top of the part, and the entire process is repeated. Laser fusion is used to create prototypes in polymer coated metal materials. A rapid prototyping process may be used for cost trade-off, cycle time, accuracy of the prototyped parts, including tolerances and surface finish, material properties, part size and part strength. This process continues to impact product development. It is the industrial trend to verify and adjust product performance and quality through rapid physical testing.

Product strategy unlike product design can be learnt the best from modern high-tech businesses and might be an idea to implement the strategy in place of design. Product strategy is like a roadmap it's useful only when you know where you are and where you want to go. A core strategic vision CSV provides the destination and the general direction to move ahead from a position in which the business stands. A 20/20 vision represents the average capability for anticipating what lies ahead. With 20/20 vision, a company can see sufficiently into the future to decide where it wants to go and how it would reach there, incorporating an understanding of technological trends and market opportunities. It is sufficient as long as the competition doesn't have better vision. Dissimilarly a company with peripheral vision is more aware of surrounding technologies, emerging brands and potential opportunities than many companies that have not honed their peripheral vision. Technologies and skills are leveraged into new markets. But it sees trends in unrelated technologies that can threaten its product platforms and market positions. By taking it further foresighted companies are able to take advantage of opportunities and parry threats that others have not yet seen. They can get the jump on competitors by developing new product platforms and solidifying skills that will be needed in the future. Bill Gates saw how quickly microprocessors would emerge and understood the need of geographical user interfaces. It is to create new software opportunities that shapes product strategies and makes them more advanced than those of competitors. Intel had been able to prove this and showed that computer users and was able to anticipate that computer users need increasing processing power, even as others believed that current processing power was more than sufficient. Intel acknowledge the ability created from Moore's law and saw that semiconductor technology would double processing power every 18 months. As a result of this foresightedness Intel developed improved microprocessors, making its own product obsolete every couple of years and dominating the market.

CSV establishes a framework for product platform strategy where generally it's the core strategic vision that initiates high level activities to replace or add a new product platform. Without a strategic vision platform strategy is unguided; a company may be at loss to decide when to launch development of a new product platform. A CSV also helps expand into new markets even if current platform and markets cannot give the firm its desired growth. It indicates the direction in which product strategy teams should look for new opportunities. With a strategic vision they begin to consider more appropriate opportunities almost subconsciously because they know generally where to look. Without a vision they come up with diverse ideas for new products that may not be consistent with the company's strength or direction. It is the primary point of strategic alignment and is important for effective execution. Every critical function, process and activity must be aligned especially if a company wants to change strategic direction. If a CSV is communicated effectively, designers don't need management to review their work to see if it is consistent. They align product development across similar projects, allowing better linking of individual products. Thus it suggests the core competences in which a company will succeed. An effective CSV can motivate people to work not just smarter but also harder. If the engineers have confidence that management knows where the company is going, and has a good vision then the business would see that the firm reaches there with the right products. A CSV boundary framework has two important purposes. It should make sure that the strategic vision is achievable. A good CSV is not impossible or unrealistic. A realistic CSV is aligned with the company's strategies, as well as the outside world-market, competition, technology trends etc. A CSV model consists of: financial model (economic model), business charter, technology trends, product strategy, market trends (competitive strategy) and core competencies (value chain). Different CSV ideas combined show that a company has strong core competencies and has a strategic vision that takes advantage of these competencies. A financial boundary enables work in the opposite direction of constraints. CSV is improvised to meet their goals for expected revenue and profit growth. CSV helps determine that a business no longer needs a particular core competency. Options include eliminating the capabilities, spinning it off into a new business, or selling it outright. In any of these cases, it is better for a company to make clear decision and communicate it rather than let the organization continue to invest in improving a core competency that is no longer needed to achieve its vision. In some cases when three internal boundary conditions and three external boundary conditions are used, most important actions are initiated by the core-competency boundary. Changes in product platform strategy, for example, are initiated through a boundary instead of a separate product strategy boundary. So the CSV boundary framework broadly establishes strategic management. Without such alignment, a company tends to follow in consistent strategies. They need to be integrated for maximum effectiveness and if they are not they can actually work against one another. One company strategically invested in a new technology that its research staff passionately believed would dramatically change all of its products. At the same time its development organization was busy perfecting and launching a new product platform based on an alternative technology. Once the company released new products based on the alternative technology. It was committed to support the technology in the marketplace; it couldn't apply the other new technology despite its superiority and availability. The alternative of licensing that new superior technology was not possible since the company didn't want the more advanced technology to be used by competitors. To thoroughly understand the impact of technology trends on the CSV, a company needs to identify the future roadmap of key technologies, emerging technologies, that could affect the future of vision and unrelated technologies that would possibly create substitute products. Major disruptive technologies broadly affect many industries, both directly and indirectly, railroads changed manufacturing and trade and transportation and thus stimulated innovation in many areas.

A product platform consists of a number of elements-frequently related to technology making different products from the platform. It is important to understand how product platforms change over time and how they differ from competitors platforms. For personal computers and workstations, the defining technology of the product platform is not the computer hardware, it is the operating system, which drives the microprocessor and interfaces with the user. The defining technology was not always obvious. The major product line of a medical products company was biological sample collection devices. They incorporated several technologies, including chemical reagents, the design and shape of the device, the gas mixture within the device and the manufacturing process to produce high quality devices. The properties required to make the device is defining technology and its properties determined the performance of the device, its cost and the shelf life and the material determines its susceptibility to breakage. The platforms unique differentiation provides a sustainable competitive advantage. Its unique differentiation is implemented primarily through the underlying product platform, not the individual products from that platform. It provides the constant theme woven throughout the product line built upon it, with individual products providing variations to the theme. It could be based on materials that have unique properties especially the products made from the Kevlar 49 platform have some clearly differentiated characteristics. They are 20% to 35% lighter than product metals. Robustness is the key element of any platform strategy. All opportunities such as proprietary technology, patents, or operational advantages should be considered as part of the strategy. Product platforms that serve a market have provoked strategic decisions in the right direction. Multiple product platforms use different underlying technology, target different market segments, and be a different point in the life cycle. A single platform may leave market opportunities open to competitors by not addressing the needs of certain segments. It takes a product platform much longer to progress through a life-cycle than the individual products derived from the platform. Platform life-cycles drive the major competitive changes in high-technology industries by introducing new product generations, forcing companies into dramatic changes in product strategy. The difficulty of replacing a product platform with a next generation platform varies considerably by the type of product. Software platforms are more easier to replace than hardware platforms, since the inventory and manufacturing issues are much simpler. Improving the underlying technology or redesigning some of the platform elements can extend the life of a limited platform. The return on the investment is limited and because of resource limitations companies frequently need to make strategic choices among platforms. Without a product line strategy, individual products will be shaped by other criteria. Instead of designing a series of product offerings for clearly defined market segments, a company will design the initial product by including all the features it believes are possible. Market segmentation should not be analyzed statically. Segmentation can change rapidly particularly in high-technology markets. As new segments emerge, product line strategy need to be modified; new product offerings may be necessary to address these newly emerging market segments. Inflexibility leads to failure when conditions change. Either the company will continue to march down a path no longer viable and the company will hop from one product to the other in an effort to catch up. Variation of product offerings within a product line is limited by the constraints of the product platform. Differentiation of the product platform is usually a primary way that a product appeals to a market segment. Ex-High performance, high-priced platform will appeal to the segment of the market willing to pay for the performance. Variations in performance and price can make a product more attractive to some market segments, but the appeal to other segments may be limited. Predictability of the timing for individual product releases is also key. If the scheduled product releases cannot be predicted accurately then the product line strategy may be questionable. An optimistic product line strategy makes one business to feel its product to have a rich feature and through predictive modeling meet the needs of a particular market segment. Taking the case of product upgrades, product upgrades are a form of add-on product important to many high-technology products, particularly computer software. Product upgrades provide additional revenue from the existing customer base, and can increase the life-cycle of many high-technology products. Once a market approaches saturation, upgrades may become the primary source of continued revenue growth. In software, some companies have implemented product line strategies based on basis of future upgrade. Technology platforms are managed differently from product platforms. Product platforms are a market faced construct and although developed collaboratively with R&D, they are managed by a business unit. Technology platforms are a core-competency for technology based companies. When a product platform cannot be applied to a new market, the underlying technology can sometimes create a new product platform. The main source is core technology. Core technology varies by product and could be critical subassemblies in an electronic systems product, or software modules in an application software product.

Leverage can also be gained from market knowledge and distribution experience. A company uses its understanding of customers and markets to design a new product that leverages this understanding. It uses its presence in the channel of distribution to bring a product to the customer the same way it has other products. Selling a new product to the existing customer base provides an opportunity to leverage both the market knowledge and the channel of distribution. Knowing what the customer wants and knowing how to sell to them can leverage in expansion. The degree of customer-base leverage depends on the breadth of the products purchased by that customer base. Expansion into a related market is easier than expansion into an unrelated market and related markets are adjacent to current markets and thus previous experience carries on. Diagonal strategy paths represents simultaneous changes in both dimensions. Diagonal strategy paths represent simultaneous changes in both dimensions. Expanding a short distance in this direction enables a company to leverage both technology and marketing thus making it a new business venture. Expansion by introducing new products into the present customer base has a low risk. It leverages its understanding both of the market and of how to sell the product, since it is already selling to the same customer base. When combined with leverage derived from using proven core technology, the result is likely to be a successful product-if the opportunity is large enough. Unique appeal to certain segments and an imperfection in the market helps make a two-dimensional snapshot of the market showing the relative positioning of competitors. Each product is more or less differentiated than others and can command a relative price reflecting the value of this differentiation. If the market does not value the differentiation of a product, then the price is usually reduced, or the product will die. It is to move a product at the upper right of the chart, while still capturing the largest market share. A company not continuously moving in this direction will drift towards lower product differentiation, and ultimately a lower price. With this average product requirements increase over time, and a company not continuously moving will drift to the bottom. Sometimes differentiation can be so significant that it creates new markets. What began as a vector of differentiation grew to be an entirely new market with its own group of competitors. The opposite can also happen. Differentiation diminishes to the point where a market based on differentiation no longer stands out from a broader market. Fault-tolerant computers are an example whereas general purpose computers became so reliable as well as less expensive that fault-tolerance was no longer supportable to a unique market. Differentiation along a vector is much better than individual points of differentiation. A vector provides the path for continuous differentiation in a specific direction. A vector of differentiation is not stagnant, it is a direction for continuous improvement. An individual point describes that it alone is a sufficient differentiation and that competitors will not catch up. There is either no need or no opportunity to go with similar type of differentiation. The next step in differentiating may be completely unrelated. Products can be differentiated in alternative directions in this step and vectors establish these directions. Products differentiated by single point have nowhere to go next and it is similar for products differentiated for multiple points and products that are differentiated in a well determined direction go very far.

In this era of E-commerce and internet pricing strategy that is a potential form of modern product strategy shows that the internet is a much lower cost distribution channel than other alternatives. The cost of providing product information is lower. Centralized inventory management is generally cheaper than inventory maintained at multiple retail locations. Internet companies sell products at a discount. The rationale is that they have cost advantages and can compete using a price leadership strategy. They also believe that volume is critical to long-term success because volume establishes the company's brand name. Generally one company can be successful as a price leader, and this can carry over to e-commerce. Only the leader has the cost advantages to support the economics of a price leadership strategy. There are definitely risks in using price as a primary offensive strategy. When a company embarks on price leadership as its primary competitive strategy, its committing to maintaining the lowest price to be successful. Risk is different in this case because there are many vectors of differentiation but only one vector of price leadership. Competing primarily on being the second lowest priced can be successful only if customers do not know the competitor's price or if the competitor is out of stock.

While looking at the sources of cost advantage traditional approaches to product design emphasize designing to a product specification that describes the product functionality, performance characteristics, operating parameters, tolerances and so on. Cost estimates are then based on the completed design and then gross margin is computed by subtracting the cost from the estimated price that the product can support. If the resulting margin is less than anticipated, the company must go back and redesign the product or proceed with the lower margins, hoping to reduce costs in the future. Thus product cost is a consequence of product design, not a requirement. When product cost is of strategic importance, it is better to use a design-to-cost approach, in which low cost is established as a product requirement of equal requirements to other critical requirements. It is an iterative process where each requirement or feature has a different cost that needs to be compared against its value. The target price and cost are linked by the required gross margin, while the price that can be charged depends on the product specifications. Manufacturing cost advantages can be derived in several ways. Economies of scale are achieved through volume, particularly when there is a high fixed cost content in the total product cost. When volume is higher, fixed costs are leveraged over many more units, reducing the cost per unit. Economies of scale is the reason why most of the companies need high volumes. Manufacturing costs can be lowered due to two reasons, including production techniques like TQM and JIT. These techniques reduce manufacturing cost by increasing quality. Vertical integration can sometimes provide a manufacturing cost advantage. If a company manufactures most of its basic materials like semiconductors, or components, it gets these at a lower cost. It reduces flexibility as technology changes and internal suppliers must be competitive with external suppliers. If not then the cost advantage turns into a disadvantage.

There are also advantages of being first to market. Whether introducing a new product platform, a more advanced product, or a new feature, the first company to market can capture additional market share simply by being first. Customers cannot buy a similar product from anyone else so there is no competition. The first company to market has a temporary monopoly. There are also other advantages. A company's reputation can be enhanced by being seen as more innovative. With enough of an advantage, a company can preempt competitors or establish barriers to entry. Competitors may see a follower strategy as less attractive, since someone has already established an advantage in the market. Being first enables a company to get earlier experience with customers, technology, suppliers and channels of distribution. The company can then use this experience to refine the product to stay ahead of competition. Being first to market provides this opportunity to get this experience before competitors. Similarly there are advantages of being the fastest. The fast product developed is nearer in time to the eventual market. There is an often overlooked advantage of faster time to market: the ability to predict what will be important in a market diminishes with the length of the prediction period. That is further ahead of the time product development starts, the more difficult the prediction, since the evolution of technology affects product differentiation, and customer expectations change. New competitive products change relative advantage, and competitive prices also change over time. While developing a new product, it must determine what the market conditions would be. It forecasts market size and price levels. It estimates the vectors of differentiation that will be preferred by the customers. It predicts the impact of technology—its own and that of competitors. A global product development process must at minimum accomplish the following: Priorities for assigning resources to new product opportunities must be determined at a global level. This is subtle, but difficult change for most companies that are used to decentralized decision making. These companies need to place product approval authority at a worldwide executive level. Moreover product marketing tasks such as product specification, competitive positioning and sales forecasting need to be done through global collaboration. It requires global collaboration of marketing and sales managers around the world. Worldwide sales organizations should be more committed to product launch and sell of product. Global product strategies are applied on an individual product platform and a company with multiple platforms can follow multiple global product strategies simultaneously. Competitive advantage can be achieved by applying a better global strategy than competitors; the catch is the degree of variation that restricts these strategies. When a low level of R&D investment is required, a global product strategy has less impact and any global strategy can be equally effective. Products designed for customers in a single country or a few directly related countries follow a regional or country specific product strategy. When a product is developed for a single country it is local or domestic strategy. Most high-technology products are the least regionally focused and developed for North American or European markets.

For acquiring a business and growing a common core strategic vision must be developed. Acquired company and acquiring company have different core strategic visions, since the reason for the acquisition for the two companies are complementary. As soon as the acquisition is complete and the CSV is revised the company should form a joint team to develop a formal marketing platform plan for senior management approval. The team and senior management should follow a well defined process so that logic rules over emotion, otherwise the differences between the two companies may become disruptive. If necessary this team should work offsite at a neutral location and get facilitation to formulate product strategy. Its worth making sure that the acquisition gets integrated into the strategy. A stronger product may capture increased market share, and revenue could grow substantially. Its important to distinguish whether a product improvement is intended as a growth strategy or not; the increase in market share will determine the direction. Growth is open to those with lower market share and might continually improve its product offerings. In certain market conditions or at certain stages of the evolution of a market, a price based strategy can be an effective highway to growth. As a price leader, a company can increase its market share and create additional revenue, as long as the relative increase in units sold, is substantially higher than relative decrease in price. In few cases aggressive pricing may also increase the size of the market by making the products more affordable to more customers. To grow through new ventures that start new products there should be an economic model that translates its business dynamics into financial terms. A new model has no baseline, so its financial plan brings its underlying economic model to life. If the business concept can be transformed into a profitable business: it generates a mathematical model of how revenue and profit will be generated from the product. It estimates how expected customers are to change over time and estimates the cost of developing and supporting new products. A new venture can sometimes use an existing core technology to build a new product platform-for example when someone develops the core technology and the new product strategy takes advantage of it to create new market. In a new market the first company creating the market must educate the market. This includes not just potential customers, but also the market infrastructure, such as press, industry analysts and investors. The concepts must be defined. For these reasons creating a new market may be slower and much more expensive then most new ventures expect. Thus portfolio management and growth through innovation and expansion strategy are the other information supplied for a business to grow.

Chapter 2

New product generation techniques through reengineering

(By Baisham Chatterjee)

The key objective behind new product planning is profitability that corresponds to a company's bottom line. Other objectives, such as company image, company awareness, customer satisfaction, and market share are common as well and these are important for long term viability or competitiveness. These efforts develop the idea of product planning. Product planning is formally defined as the process of envisioning, conceptualizing, developing, producing, testing, commercializing, sustaining and disposing of organizational efforts to satisfy organizational needs and wants and achieve organizational objectives. Product planning is certainly a broad and complex endeavor, comprising numerous issues and activities many of which are cross-disciplinary. Product planning consists of two types product development and product management. In product development a product or service is conceived, developed, produced or tested. It is a up-front process. Product management is a back-end process where the product or service is commercialized, sustained and eventually withdrawn.

Product planning serves various key roles in the company. One of these roles is resource allocation. Product planning analyzes each product or service whether current or new, to determine the resources to be successful and increase the impact for the company. Related to the role of resource allocation is that of product mix co-ordination. This determines that a particular type of product is not overwhelming the company's offerings or diluting the customers interests. The most important idea is to provide a product mix possibility. Another role is marketing program support where based on current performance of existing firms product planning can provide correct information. Another method is the appraisal of company offerings. In this the impact on the business can be understood by evaluating the performance of current products or services. The impact is measured in terms of cash flow. Products are found to be either generating a profit or losing money from the company. Product planners consider how to increase the profit being generated and in the latter product planners consider actions needed to turn the product around. Product planners identify products that should be deleted and chart a course of action for proper termination of the product. This includes programs to transition customers for alternative products, and a plan to maintain a spare parts inventory for the product being deleted so as to not alienate customers of the product.

Innovations are those that creates products and they are basically inventions around which a marketing program has been built to clearly offer a benefit to customers, and a benefit that satisfies a market need, want or desire. Innovations can be classified as continuous and discontinuous innovations. Continuous innovation involves slight product changes and such innovations are a result of normal upgrading of products and do not require a change in customer behavior. Discontinuous innovations revolutionize the market infrastructure, making other technologies obsolete and changing the lifestyle of consumers. An example of discontinuous innovation is fusion powered vehicles. A product line is a group of closely related product items and distinguishing both is influenced by a variety of reasons. It indicates a new opportunity and helps spread resources in a more optimal fashion. Product lines also can serve as a signal about quality and thus can aid in gaining market acceptance as well as promoting product items. Three characteristics are used to describe the product mix: width, depth and consistency. Width represents the number of different product lines. A wide product mix suggests many product lines whereas a narrow product mix suggests very few product lines. Consistency is the degree of commonality among lines with respect to end use, distribution outlets, consumer groups or price range. It would suggest similar product lines and an inconsistent product mix would suggest a diverse mix of product lines.

An issue faced by product planners is product proliferation. It describes the current trend of companies to expand the width and depth of their mixes. Product planners, therefore need an explosion of product items that need to be managed. Even with use of product platforms, product proliferation makes product planning more difficult. New to the world products are technological innovations that creates a completely new market that previously did not exist. These innovations would be characterized as a discontinuous innovation. The introduction of the first commercial cellular phone is an example of new to the world products. Companies do not deal with one type of new product, rather multiple types of new products permeate the product planning process. New product success measures can be generalized into four different categories: customer-based measures, competitive based measures, financial measures and technical performance. Customer based success can be based on customer satisfaction, customer acceptance, unit volume and number of repeat customers. Competitive based measures includes market share, competitive benchmarking and competitive advantage. Financial measures can be revenue, profit, margin, rate of return and payback. A market penetration strategy for a new product is based on an objective to increase market share or increase product usage. The current customer base is pursued with no major changes to the existing product technology. Cost improvements and product improvements are characteristic to a market penetration strategy. A product development strategy derives from an objective to capitalize on new product technology and offer more options to the customer base. Thus the company with a more diverse product line can fend off competitors.

Interestingly, product development processes are similar across companies and industries: commonalities can be found regardless of the underlying philosophical principles that created the process. Indeed most product development processes would reflect similar stages: opportunity identification, concept generation, pre-technical evaluation, technical development and launch. One common shortcoming is the omission of the sixth product development stage, life cycle management, which should be considered and which some companies include as part of the product development process. Opportunity identification represents the first stage of the product development process. The purpose of this stage is to delineate a direction for the product development initiative. Amore formal approach for getting approved is to prepare a product development charter, also referred to as a product innovation charter, which would then be approved when moving to the next stage. Concept generation is the second stage that puts together a set of new product ideas/ concepts generated. This can facilitate the effort for concept generation. Some companies conduct concept generation prior to opportunity identification. These companies which follow this principle prefer to begin the process with a clean slate, providing an environment for greater innovation. Pre-technical evaluation is the third stage where product concepts are evaluated and prioritized. This stage is a business analysis of the product concept. This concept shows the growing potential to meet company objectives and goals are further defined via product protocols. The fourth stage is the product development process where the technology behind the product concept is realized and tested to ensure that it meets the specifications in the product protocol. Construction of a viable business/ marketing plan also occurs. This assesses whether a tangible product has been developed and functions as desired. The financial viability and marketability of the product also is gauged to make a determination of whether to commit resources and continue work on the product. Next is the launch stage that consists of market acceptance of the new product, including market testing, prelaunch preparation and post-launch control. The sixth stage of the product development process is the lifecycle management. It includes continuous monitoring, possible refinement of the launched product and the possible augmentation of the product to create a product line.

There are many ways of designing product safety which are through-designing products to be fail-safe, allow for human error, avoid sharp corners, ground electrical products properly and look at all the safety measures. Minimize as much as possible the use of flammable materials, including packaging material. Develop products that do not require heavy or prolonged operations to avoid the kind of user actions that can lead to trauma disorders such as carpal tunnel syndrome. It is important to design the product for easy testability where it is important that as much as possible design the product and its components so that tests can be made with standard instruments. Incorporate built in-test capability and if possible, built in self testing devices in the product. Make the tests standardized to help it perform in the field. Provide accessibility for test probes, ex-prominent test points or access holes for test probes and make modules testable while still assembled to the product. There are different types of product testing like alpha testing, beta testing, gamma testing. Alpha testing is an in-house testing where employees serve as the basis of testing and it is less expensive and competitors are not tipped to the new product. This doesn't necessarily reflect customer views. Beta testing looks at the customer operations and the customer site. The customer provides insight into the product and its functioning. Gamma testing is a longer term test where the product is put through extensive use by the customer and predominantly used by pharmaceutical companies to the regulatory issues surrounding medicinal drugs. Al though there are risks of product use testing these are some of the important aspects of product use testing.

After the product testing is done and determined through assemblies and other techniques, new product forecasting techniques might be used to make the marketing techniques better. They are another set of tools that are used during the launch cycle, as well as earlier in the product development process. During the launch cycle a company's production distribution systems would use certain forecasting techniques to prepare for launch: the first is Box-Jenkins technique that involves time series and regression-model building. The major characteristics are identifying, determining and testing the model. Other forecasting techniques are market research and decision trees. Decision trees are a probabilistic approach to forecasting. Diffusion models estimate the growth rate of product sales by considering various factors that influence consumers adopting a product. They are employed for new product forecasting. Experience curves forecasting using experience curves assumes that as cumulative production volume of a product rises, the cost of producing each unit falls according to the predictable curve. Expert systems through setting rules and if-then principle and exponential smoothing techniques are other ways of determining the new product launch. There are many more methods like: looks-like analysis which attempts to map sales of other products onto the product being forecast. Market analysis models like the ATAR model, assumptions-based models. Market analysis models attempt to model the behavior of the relevant market environment by breaking the market down into market drivers. Moving average, neural networks, non-linear regression and correlation method are other techniques. Scenario analysis, simulation and trend line analysis are other techniques.

PLM or product lifecycle management is driven in waves. PLM eliminates waste and efficiency and is focused on using power of information and computers to deliberate pare inefficiencies from the design, manufacturing, support and ultimate disposal of a product. PLM uses product information, computers, software and simulations to produce the first product as efficiently and as productively as the last product throughout the design, development and delivery process. PLM holds the promise of improving productivity through a cross-functional approach using product information. By linking different functional areas through shared information, PLM can help organizations break down the silo perspective and unlock productivity gains as functional areas benefit from a shared base of information. As supply chains become more integrated, PLM has the potential for impact across these supply chains-not just within the organization. The other allure of PLM is that it does not improve efficiency and productivity from simply a cost reduction perspective. Increasing costs are not an inherent bad thing. If revenues are increasing, it is almost impossible not to increase costs.

The general idea is that as organizations gain experience with producing and manufacturing a product, their unit production costs generally decrease over time. These cost decreases are not simply because of information learned by the production workers who are actually producing the product. Other areas of the organization, such as engineering, purchasing and administration also participate in generating the cost decreases. Even organizations where the manufacturing or production process is highly automated so that learning from the manufacturing or production process is substantially limited still show cost decreases with cumulative unit production. Product lifecycle management is an advanced outlook of reengineering where it is an integrated information driven approach to all aspects of a products life, from its design through manufacture, deployment and maintenance-culminating in the product's removal from service and final disposal. PLM software suites enable accessing, updating, manipulating, and reasoning about product information that is being produced in a fragmented and distributed environment. Since information does not degrade, the duration of the information about a physical product is not an issue. However, the hardware and software systems that store and access the information are another matter. Hardware and software systems become obsolete and unsupported and media degrades. PLM has signed up for a task of long duration. From an implementation standpoint, it is too early to determine whether PLM can meet the challenge and whether, as advances in hardware and software occur, the old information can migrate along with these advances. PLM is about the product. It is not related to supply chains or domain expertise. PLM is all about the product and its associated information. PLM encompasses such effects like strategy, philosophy why we organize information and shows that what we really mean over here is technology.

The main focus of PLM generally is on new product development. It is a fairly logical proposition for an organization to start a major new initiative at the beginning of its lifecycle of its new products. Some organizations might load existing items into PLM applications, but it will probably be more for the reason that these items can be used as components of new products than for the reason they can be used in other phases of the lifecycle such as sales and service. The state of the art in PLM applications has been focused on the new product development area. Certain technologies for PLM offerings have been in development and use for many years. Software applications and other product lifecycle aspects like product's lifecycle, such as manufacturing, sales and support and disposal are recent introductions and are relatively immature. There are compelling business reasons for focusing on the NPD & I area. Around 80% of the cost structure of a product is defined as the requirements definition and engineering stage of a new products development. To sense the focus on this area of the product's lifecycle when its lifetime cost structure can be impacted.

The build of a product has three fairly distinct phases: building the first product, ramping production up and building the rest of the products. In manufacturing the first product there are two considerations: building it in a new plant, building it in an existing plant. In building the product in a new plant, the design phase just got substantially more complicated, because not only must the product be designed, but the tools must be specified. Manufacturing engineers can send request for quotations (RFQs) to tool manufacturers to ask them to provide quotes on building tools that will meet those specifications. Software applications that implement PLM must have as a fundamental characteristic the ability to manage this singularity of the product data. PLM systems must have the ability to identify the controlling product data so that there is no question, if there are multiple versions which is the one that everyone refers to. The fundamental purpose of PLM is to expend time, energy and material in reconciling different versions of the product data and redoing the work that cannot be reconciled. There is a cost to collecting data from the tangible object, the time, energy, and sometimes material to disassemble, measure, weigh etc.

The next element of PLM information characteristics is cohesion. Cohesion means that there are going to be different representations or views of product information depending on perspectives of the product.

There is always a geometrical or mechanical view of the product in our minds. This mechanical view is a geometrical, three-dimensional view of the product. It shows the three-dimensional space hidden surfaces and cross-sections. Many products have an electrical view, which is the logic diagram or schematic that shows the electrical system contained within the product. The length of the visual lines connecting electrical components has no relationship to the length of the actual wires that are required to physically connect these components within the product. This logical view of the electrical system must eventually be represented in physical components. Wires must be run. Specific chips must either be selected or designed. Voltage sources must be bought and installed in the product. If the electrical schematic changes because someone realizes that it would not produce the desired function, then the physical implementation also must change. If a physical component changes that will change the functionality of the electric system, then the electrical view must change to reflect that. This is cohesiveness.

The physical product obviously has the superior position. The logic diagram can be changed as much as we can produce certain functionality. Requisite components and wiring are needed to make a product perfect. The functionality of the physical product is determined by atoms not bits. If the product's functionality is mirrored in virtual space there needs to be a cohesion between views. Cohesion is not a problem in the real space, but in real space there is information about the product as part of its very makeup. In virtual space in different computer programs: one view is for geometrical representation, one view is for electrical schematic representation, one for hydraulic system representation and one for BOM.

Traceability is the ability to demonstrate that the path of a product's travel through time can be followed seamlessly back to its origin. The reason that traceability is important is that we continually put our ideas, designs, and products to test to determine whether or not our assumptions about the attributes and functionality of the three factors are disproved. We can rely on the tests only in two situations. The first is if we are referencing the unchanged version we tested. The second is if we are referencing derivatives of that version where we have high confidence that we can understand how the changes affect the attributes and functionality and where we can compute with a required degree of confidence new test results that would mirror the actual tests if we were to perform them. Due to lack of traceability time, energy and material might be wasted. After building on the unsuccessful version and wasting a little bit of the time, energy and material we understand that we chose the wrong one. It is clear that the scale of companies is dramatically increasing, and has increased over a period of time and most likely will continue its increase into the future. PLM systems are not only a luxury but a requirement. If information systems are driving these companies to be able to substitute information for wasted time, energy and material and to deal with increasing amounts of information accurately and reliably. These rapid scaling companies have derivative effects on the companies that they do business with. They impact smaller companies and these rapid scaling companies understand that the information requirements do not start and stop within these four walls, and they are extending their informational requirements out through the supply chain.

The design cycle is somewhere between two and three years, and the pressure is on to decrease that time-frame. Automotive companies are taking an 18 month cycle and even early years in terms of introducing new products. Decreasing cycle time are not confined to durable goods with historically long lead times. In case of the clothing and fashion industry the cycle time has been reduced from 90 days to lesser than 60 days. Decreasing cycle times have a dual impact. First they substantially increase the amount of information that needs to be collected, processes, accessed and stored. Even if decreased development cycle times mean decreased life-cycle times, which may not be true as product's durability improves, the information about the product needs to be accessible for an extended period of time because of rules and regulations regarding serviceability, regulatory, and /or litigation requirements. Second, decreasing cycle time means the elimination of slack that previously existed to coordinate different uses of different functional areas, reconcile differences brought on by the use of inconsistent information, or keep usage in synchronization. Decreasing cycle time means that the usual mechanism for dealing with disparate information-the coordination or review meeting where the project would stop while all parties check pointed their progress and compared their individual progress to their overall progress-which is a luxury in time which most organizations can no longer afford. Organizations cannot afford the time to check point and resynchronize their efforts. PLM is the new mechanism that facilitates this change in methods due to this ever-decreasing cycle times. As a result local firms in developing countries can acquire, deploy and support the sophisticated capabilities of PLM. Organizations in developing countries are gaining the efficiencies that accompany the breakdown of barriers between functional areas and the sharing of product information in a comprehensive fashion. They are doing so with their lower labor cost advantage, although that may be compensated for somewhat by their disadvantage of scale.

The theory of productivity is becoming universal and the complexity of coordination increases as work is distributed to far-flung and constantly changing geographical locations. That would also normally increase costs to counterbalance the decrease in wage rate. However PLM provides this co-ordination through the availability of product information. PLM helps capture this source of increased productivity by moving the required information about the product to wherever the work moves and to integrate the new, lower cost workforce with the use of same processes and practices employed by the previous workforce. Taking the case of innovation where productivity is concerned with the cost side of the organization, product innovation addresses the revenue side. Without product innovation an organizations revenue stream is at risk of declining, if not ceasing altogether. Once-successful companies that fail to continue to innovate are overtaken by companies that introduce new and innovative products into their market space. While innovation of product form is not to be underestimated-people seek and reward visual changes-the innovation of product function is the innovation that is the goal of all organizations.

Novel products functions that create real value for their users by reducing the time, energy and material required to perform tasks or by enabling their users to do tasks not previously possible are the innovations that organizations should focus on creating.

In the IT value map, there are only two ways to increase income. The first is to increase revenue. The second is to decrease cost. If we look at the revenue side of the IT Value map, revenue consists of two components. One component is the price of the product that the organization is producing. The other component is the quantity of products sold. All things being equal, the price of the product is dependent on the quality of that product and the amount of functionality that the product has. Higher the productivity higher the price. A company with declining quality can see the price for its product decrease. Organization's are simply buying two things: people's time at a specified rate and material at a specified cost. When the organizations are buying material, they are rarely just purchasing material alone. Included in the purchase price of the material is the time of the supplier's people multiplied by a wage rate, plus-hopefully for that supplier's shareholders-a profit. This relationship continues down the supply chain. Direct costs usually come with a multiplier. Overhead percentages are usually relatively stable with respect to direct costs. When we add direct costs, we also eventually add a percentage of indirect costs for every dollar of direct costs we add. We add costs such as more supplies, more space and more material. We also add people at their time multiplied by their rate. These people process the new payroll, sell the additional products produced by the new people, bill for new revenue, manage the new people.

What lean manufacturing does is to decrease the amount of time that people waste on efficient tracks. Lean manufacturing is an integral part of PLM and its attempts to decrease the amount of wasted material due to the production of incorrect or excess product. Thus lean manufacturing has a good value proposition for the organizations that take on lean manufacturing projects because it can decrease wasted time and material. On the cost side ERP is primarily a manufacturing and sales system and its impact unlike lean manufacturing is to decrease the amount of time and wasted material that people spend on the project. However ERP systems are generally very expensive. The increase in income through the decrease in cost and increase in revenue is offset by the substantial increase in assets and are deployed to implement an ERP system. PLM gives the information that enables people to reduce the time spent on developing products that already exist. People can work on improved versions that minimize manufacturing costs and are easily serviced. By using virtual space to better design, validate and test their products, organizations can have a higher confidence level that their products will perform for their users the way they are supposed to. Products that perform as well or better than users expect are the real definition of the test of quality. Increasing market share results in an increase in the quality of units sold and is a natural consequence of better quality and functionality. As the left side of the IT Value map says that, the creation of the value of PLM is not only a function of the increase in income through reduced costs and improved revenues. It is dependent on the relation of this improvement in income to the investment in PLM. The investment in PLM is not insignificant. For large organizations it can easily run in the millions of dollars to acquire software, hardware and consulting services and change management, education and training. However unlike ERP, which requires up-front commitment of millions of dollars worth of resources to support this initiative, PLM can be phased on a project-by-project basis. This means that even when the organization develops an overall PLM strategy covering the spectrum of PLM capabilities, it can implement that strategy in distinct initiatives, ranking the initiatives on their individual returns and making the necessary investments overtime. PLM solution providers, as they attempt to reach more and more organizations, are unbundling their applications so that smaller organizations can acquire and implement affordable subsets of PLM.

Capturing and categorizing exemplars of practice is also a function that PLM can enable. This will increase the pool of information that will enhance judgmental decision making. Decisions that can be reduced to unambiguous rules belong in processes. The decisions that cannot be reduced to unambiguous rules belong in practices. Decisions involved in practices have as their goal relatively clear objectives or output. Inputs and mechanisms required to produce the inputs to take decisions are fuzzy and often not well understood. The reason that this may be the case is that human beings are superb at comparison and pattern recognition. However in order to do this, they need information to compare against and patterns that can be recognized. PLM can assist in practice by categorizing and providing exemplars of past decisions. If we have these exemplars available, we can use them to compare against our current decision. If designers have exemplars of designs that were both approved and rejected, they can use them to make decisions about their designs. If manufacturing engineers have exemplars have example of successful and unsuccessful manufacturing processes, they may be able to find commonalities with their proposed processes and weed out once those patterns are similar to failed processes.

PLM brings to bear on the problem is its ability to enforce singularity of information. By assigning a part number and mapping it to a specific and hopefully unique set of specifications about a product, we are attempting to simplify information processing and communication across the organization. If there is a singularity of information that is accessible to everyone, then a part number maps to a specific set of specifications and characteristics. Difference can be resolved by compromising on a common specification or by creating a new part number. PLM will not inherently stop the proliferation of the identical specifications and characteristics with different part numbers. In case of the collaboration room for the PLM the project board already exists in the form of the workflow management tools that exist within all cPD applications. Task assignments, task statuses, routings, sign offs and other product development information are generally one of the first implementations of PLM. It is much better than a passive project board in that these PLM applications are proactive. They notify participants of task assignments and deadlines and alert product development team members of new requirements, changes and missed deadlines. As a further benefit all product development activities can be aggregated to give senior leadership a comprehensive view of all the development activities within an organization. The last requirement of the collaboration room is that it captures the changes to the product as the development progresses. Traceability is a key characteristic of PLM and, by the electronic nature of the collaboration room, a history and a audit trail of changes can easily be captured and retained. This is an advantage over physical meetings, where the way decisions were made is often lost. Electronic mediation-people using computers to communicate with one another-provides a mechanism for capturing not only the final decision, but the considerations and criteria involving the final decision.

Mock-ups and prototypes allows product designers and engineers to gather around a real, tangible object; walk around it; look over it; and examine from any possible perspective the design as it would actually take shape. For mock-ups of exterior surfaces, clay was and still is the choice for rendering large-scale objects, although plastic is often used for smaller objects and components. The purpose of these models is primarily to examine the visual and aesthetic features of the design, although they are also used to assess surface issues of manufacturability due to surfaces requiring too many or too steep changes in direction. Prototypes, which are full-scale geometric replicas that may or may not be operable, require craft production since they are literally one-of-a-kind objects. Prototypes are used to assess fit-and finish of exterior surfaces and other components that must be assembled and fit together. Prototypes are used to assess compatibility of design criteria-for example, looking for fuel lines that are too close to heat sources in automobile and aircraft, or too near magnetic fields in medical diagnostic equipments. They are used in assessing the visual and manual accessibility of instruments. Prototypes also provide an opportunity for manufacturing engineers to assess manufacturability and assembly issues. There is human assembly involved in assembly:

getting under the prototype, reaching in to connect one part to another, connecting wiring harness through access points. Both mock-ups and prototypes are consuming to build. They are expensive. They expend wall clock time and introduce lags into the development process. In rapid prototyping, a substantial amount of prototypes require expensive tooling to be built, which might be discarded if the design changes because of or in spite of the prototype. Savings can be enormous if fewer mock-ups and prototypes are built later in the design cycle, because information can be substituted for the physical objects.

The challenge of ramp up is more than simply driving down the experience or learning curve. Manufacturing ramp up of new products is invariably accompanied by product changes, commonly referred to as ECOs (Engineering change orders). ECOs disrupt the drive down the experience of learning curve. These ECOs can introduce inefficiencies into the production process that increase costs to a point higher than the production was initially started, because the initial production method has to be unlearned and a new method learned. Production machinery has to be taken down, reprogrammed and debugged. PLM has an entire approach in general and Digital Manufacturing should reduce the amount of ECOs required. According to the CIM Data, companies utilizing PLM have reported an astounding 65% reduction in ECOs. Increased ability in the design and engineering function to determine if the product design actually delivers the desired functionality reduces the need for ECOs. The designers and engineers can determine that their product designs actually function as expected, not just looking like the intended design. This should reduce the instances of functionality failing to materialize or unintended functionality cropping up. The ECO introduction can be simulated to determine the least disruptive method of installation. Automated equipment in the case of digital manufacturing can be reprogrammed and debugged in virtual space.

PLM is a logical part of a strategy to increase revenues and lower costs. PLM decreases costs through Lean Thinking, trading off material for wasted time, energy, material. The resources freed up can drive an increase in product variety, quantity, functionality and quality. One technique in use to develop a vision of tomorrow is to bring the senior leadership together and ask them to imagine themselves, say, five years in the future, then look around and describe what they see. PLM in particular, benefits from an approach like this because some of the unintended benefits from collecting and sharing information might not be obvious. It is only when we take a new and discontinuous look at the future that we might perceive novel and creative uses of information that are not simply extrapolations of what we have done in the past. PLM not only is compatible with the "One Company" vision that not only reduces costs but increases the revenue, but is also a means to implement it by building a substructure of product information that all the operations and their functions can share. In addition where this product substructure is shared with the supplier community, these suppliers are also structured by being part of these processes and practices sharing from this common base of production.

In PLM, the danger with respect to resource allocation is the Goldilocks effect, asking for too much or too little. Because PLM can have such a large reach and impact within the organization, there can be a tendency to develop a comprehensive vision of tomorrow and a desire to allocate the entire resources to enable the plan to accomplish this. The larger the request, more detailed the plan and there is greater confidence in the outcomes and decision makers. Requesting too small a resource allocation means that PLM would be viewed as peripheral and unimportant. There can be some of the practice aspects of PLM such as rich communication or instant messaging. PLM can impact both costs and revenues across the organization, it should compare well with other initiatives and should be a priority to fund. If venture capitalists or bankers can be convinced that value can be created, organizations should be able to provide the justification for PLM. Change is difficult enough, but coupling it with the introduction of new technology amplifies the problem. The change and technology requirements of PLM are of a nature that organizational leadership cannot simply approve the plan and sit back waiting for status reports. Breaking new ground in developing a substructure product information that becomes a new major asset of the organization is groundbreaking work. Since PLM is an evolving area, the vision of the future will also surely evolve. The external drivers of changing scale, scope, complexity, cycle time, and regulatory pressures, the probability of organization leaders will have 20/20 vision of the future is remote if not completely non-existent. The positions of PLM that create other initiatives are: PLM is for creating a valuable asset to the organization, namely intellectual property concerning the products of the organization. This is in addition to showing real cost savings and revenue opportunities. However with PLM it is critical that members of the team have both deep knowledge and understanding of their departments and functions and the ability to make decision for their organization without having to go back and seek permission from other managers.

It is also imperative that team members be decision makers. PLM is not a matter of implementing the status quo. It requires fundamental changes in how the organization views its processes and practices. If team members are not decision makers, valuable time and effort will be lost because team members will have to go back to their respective organizations and attempt to explain why reallocation of resources is necessary. For PLM to be successful tem members must work on right allocation of resources, make decisions within the committee room and then be able to execute on those decisions and implement them. PLM is a different way of doing things, especially as it pertains to crossing functional boundaries. Thus change management of new processes and practices need to be closely interlinked with the project management. Similarly taking the case of information and communication which builds all this, the PLM system will be installed with the replacement system or will b integrated with the current in-use systems. It is difficult to understand the information flows but it should be integrated to the current system. PLM system is going to integrate with current systems, then the problem is lessened because they can be linked or integrated into the new system.

To bring the idea of PLM to a success organizational reengineering has to be involved to structure the problem and complexity. It involves re-organizing work flows, cutting waste, combining process steps and eliminating repetitive tasks. This will not work with the corporate culture. The process sets aside the traditional culture and presents a new set of organizational principles. It involves finding new ways and developing new rules that would help take a quantum leap. Reengineering can be applied, to new product development processes which turn an idea into a manufacturable and marketable prototype. Customers can be internal as the end points of success, such as department or group or something external to the organization. Customers are the ultimate judges for quality and process output. A physical transformation changes some tangible item, such as semi-finished material, into another state. Locational transformation is another thing that changes physical items. Transactional transformation involves the modification of non-tangible items that includes the electronic movement of money in banks, the sales of stock by stockbrokers or the assembly of market research data for starting a new innovation process. Feedback involves communication and evaluation channels, by which transformation activities are modified or corrected to maintain desired attributes of output. Feedback can take the form of economic information such as gross sales revenue which is used to evaluate the operation. Making a process evaluation a process owner must be identified and designated, and customer-supplier relationships and requirements both internal and external to the process. Measurements of effectiveness and efficiency must be identified and put in place. The process must be assessed and deficiencies or exposures such as defects, rework, excess cost, redundancies or supplier problems must be identified. The process must be competitive both in terms of effectiveness and efficiency as compared with comparable processes within the organization or industry. The process must be adaptable to business-direction changes without loss of efficiency and must be deemed by the customer to be able to meet requirements for several years. Similarly in the case of information flows that is the most important case of pipelines. A pipeline moves a single package of information or material between the activities, files and external entities. Two separate pipelines moves between two activities. It is thus no two pipelines have the same name, pipelines that move into and out of files do not require names, and the file name will suffice to describe the pipeline. The thick line vectors often represents a flow of physical material from process to process, such as movement of tape from storage facility to a tape silo. However some IFD creators use manufacturing pipelines to show the principal flow and support pipelines show scheduling and production control. In the case of production control it is important to assess the gaps, then develop pilot objectives, develop pilot measures, gain agreement from stakeholders, conduct a pilot of the new process, assess the impact of the pilot process for desired results and then implement the new process. Before the pilot process the idea thought of is developing a work plan by depicting the process in a flow chart through an integrated flow diagram that would help complete the process-mapping worksheet, complete the process-constraint analysis, that would help complete the cultural factor analysis to create the ideal process. In case of process mapping it is first important to determine the critical organization process and then measuring the critical process and then rate the process performance to orient the process sponsor and then define the preliminary opportunity, assess the limitations of the opportunity, set preliminary project goals to discuss a timetable that would finally establish the scope of a process-mapping project. Thus product lifecycle and product planning are only successful only when these particular points are taken into view and an organization is reengineered.

Chapter 3

Manufacturing strategy and revolutionizing product development

(BY BAISHAM CHATTERJEE)

Different companies within the same industry compete in different ways. The measurements of competition are in price, quality, product innovation, rapid delivery and customer service that use different yardsticks of success. The task for a company's manufacturing function is to create a production system that through a series of interrelated and internally consistent choices, reflects the priorities and trade-offs implicit in its specific competitive situation and strategy. The most dysfunctional thing is the view that the manufacturing function is being managed effectively as long as production costs are kept low and sufficient capacity is being available to meet demand. The fiercest competition in manufacturing is not based on better product design, marketing ingenuity, or financial strength as on something much harder to duplicate: superior overall manufacturing capability. To minimize manufacturing's negative potential outside experts are called in to make decisions about strategic manufacturing issues with the internal detailed management control systems as the primary means for monitoring manufacturing performance with the manufacturing kept as flexible and reactive. In the second stage it is important to achieve parity with competitors where industry practice is followed. The planning horizon for manufacturing investment decisions is extended to incorporate a single business cycle. Capital investment is the primary means for catching up with competition or achieving a competitive edge. It is also important to provide credible support to the business strategy where manufacturing investments are screened for consistency with the business strategy and a manufacturing strategy is formulated and pursued. Longer-term manufacturing and trends are addressed systematically.

Efforts are made to anticipate the potential of new manufacturing practices and technologies and manufacturing is involved in major marketing and engineering decisions. Long-range programs are pursued in order to acquire capabilities in advance of needs.

Every manufacturing operation embodies a set of important choices about such factors as capacity, vertical integration, human resource policies. A given operation is composed of factors that are themselves at different levels of development. What determines the overall level of this operation is where the balance among these factors falls-that is, where in the developmental scheme the operations centre of gravity rests. Organizations typically view manufacturing capability as the direct result of a few structural decisions about capacity, facilities, technology and vertical integration. Managers attach little or no strategic importance to such infrastructure issues as workforce policies, planning and measurement systems and incremental process improvements. When strategic issues involving manufacturing arises, management usually calls in outside experts in the belief that its own production organization lacks the necessary expertise. In high-tech companies when the manufacturing may appear clumsy and unprepared when confronted with straightforward tasks as adequate production capacity, helping suppliers solve problems and keeping equipment and systems up to date.

Automation is essential-not just to reduce costs but also to improve quality. Modifications in product design had to reflect the capabilities and constraints of the new process. That process has to accommodate more worker control and shorter manufacturing cycle times, along with other non-traditional approaches to improve flexibility, quality, delivery dependability, and the integration of product testing with manufacturing. In the case of IBM reaching the low-cost position required stabilizing the manufacturing environment and linking manufacturing more effectively to marketing and distribution. The emphasis on direct costs which attends the productivity focus, leads a company to use management controls and focus on the wrong targets. These controls key on direct labor: overhead is allocated to direct labor; variances from standards are calculated from direct labor. Performance in customer service, delivery, lead times, quality and asset turns are secondary. The reward systems based on such controls drives behavior towards simplistic goals that represent only a small fraction of total costs while the real costs lie in overhead and purchased material. Managers in flexible factories have broadened the concept of service to include both a commitment to product variety and a capacity to see the customer in specialized terms. The ability to produce small lot sizes efficiently and to change quickly from one product to another is the flexibility key. The most flexible factories are not capitalizing on the full range of services they could provide. Factories generate information and skill that are critical for product design. Among them are accurate and timely feedback on manufacturability of new designs, the ability to construct prototypes quickly, and the capability for introducing engineering change orders smoothly. But factories are also a resource for helping customers with installation, maintenance and troubleshooting. The people who made products are often more knowledgeable about the performance, variability, and repair than the people in field service. The aim of being a dispatcher and creating a customer linkage can be achieved in several ways. In the most innovative approach sometimes called inter-organizational systems, factories supply customers with computer terminals that are linked directly to the factory's order entry and production control system. Even without sophisticated information systems customer linkages can be tightened through inter-functional teams consisting of representatives from sales, logistics and manufacturing. Laboratory, consultant, showroom and dispatcher shows a distinctive approach to factory service. Manufacturing managers sought to maximize efficiency and protect the line from outside disturbances; they buffered themselves by storing inventories in locations that were set off from the rest of the organization and from customers. The relationship between standardization and flexibility may have to change whenever the product, process or distribution changes. Switching from selling heavy equipment to leasing it may drastically change the ratio between finished products output and spare parts output. A minor model change where major parts are assembled into the finished product, but under traditional line such changes are ignored. With product life cycles shortening all the time and competition intensifying such changes cannot be ignored.

In the new manufacturing business, manufacturing is the integrator that ties everything together. It creates the economic value that pays for everything and everybody. Thus the greatest value on the manufacturing systems concept will not be on the production process. As with SQC, its greatest impact will be on social and human concerns-or career ladder, or more important, on the transformation of functional managers into business managers, each with a specific role. In continuous improvement systems, tightly linked teams bridge disparate functions that typically interact with each other in a predictable sequential manner. A hallmark is the conviction that every process must contribute to satisfying the customer by constantly and incrementally achieving higher quality. It has a big difference with mass-customizing systems is that workers do not question the basic design of the product that they are assigned to build; they assume it to be what customers want. Continuous improvement organizations school workers in tools and techniques help them improve the task they must perform. These managers strive to tighten the link between processes so that every team and individual worker knows how its function affects others and ultimately the products and service. Mass customization on the other hand requires a dynamic network or relatively autonomous operating units. Outside suppliers and vendors do not come together all the time. From continually trying to meet these demands, the mass customization learns what new capabilities it requires. Its employees are on the quest to improve their own skills, as well as those of the unit and network, in a never ending campaign to expand the number of ways the company can satisfy customers.

There are two distinct organization forms: The mechanistic organization, so named because of the management emphasis on automating tasks and treating workers like machines consists of a bureaucratic structure of functionally defined highly compartmentalized jobs. Organic organization is so named because of its fluid and ever changing nature, is characterized by an adaptable structure of loosely defined jobs. In continuous improvement companies where workers are encouraged to think about their jobs and how processes can be improved, technology is primarily used to augment workers knowledge and skills. Measurement and analysis programs, computerized decision support systems, videoconferencing, and even machine tools are aids, not people replacements. In the dynamic network of mass customizers, technology still automates tasks where that makes sense. Certainly technology must augment people's knowledge and skills, but the elements of mass customization require that technology automates the link between modules and ensure that people and tools necessary to perform them are brought together instantly. Communication networks, shared databases that let everyone view the customer information simultaneously, computer integrated manufacturing, workflow software and tools like groupware can automate the links so that the company can summon exactly the right resources. There are a lot of common standards for measuring manufacturing performance. Among these are short delivery cycles, superior product quality and reliability, dependable delivery promises, ability to produce new products quickly, flexibility in adjusting to volume changes, low investments and hence high return on investment and low costs. These measures of manufacturing performance necessitate trade-offs-where certain tasks must be compromised to meet others. They cannot all be accomplished equally well because of the inevitable limitations of equipment and process technology. Such trade-offs as costs versus quality or short delivery cycles versus low inventory investment are fairly obvious. Other trade-offs involve implicit choices in establishing manufacturing policies. Therefore the choice of focus and of course production people is a result of the comprehensive analysis of company's resources, strengths and weaknesses, position in the industry, assessment of competitors moves and forecast of future customer motives and behavior.

It is seen that capital investment in new equipment is essential to sustaining growth over a long time. Simply investing money in new technology or systems guarantees nothing. What matters is how their introduction is managed, as well as the extent to which they support and reinforce continual improvement throughout a factory. Managed right, new investment supports cumulative long term productivity improvement and process understanding. Many small changes in product design, machinery and operating practices are made as they gain experience. Seeking new business as the business redesigns an established product and purchases the equipment required to make it. This new equipment was similar to the plants existing machinery but its introduction allowed for enhancing changes in work flows. Plant managers discovered how the new configuration could accommodate expanded production without a proportional increase in work force. The real boost in the new equipment came not only from the equipment itself but also from the opportunities it provided to search for and apply new knowledge to the overall production process. Investment unfreezes old assumptions, generates more efficient concepts and designs for a production system and expands a factory's skills and abilities. New equipment usually causes problems. Everyone expects a temporary drop in efficiency as equipment is installed and workers learn to use it. But managers often underestimate the costly ripple effects of new equipment on inventory, quality, equipment utilization, reject rates, downtime and material waste. Indeed these indirect costs often exceed the direct cost of the new equipment and can persist for more than a year after the equipment is installed.

Design engineers take for granted environmental forces degrading performance. They try to counter this effect in product designs-insulating wires, adjusting tire treads, sealing joints. Performance degradations of these may arise either from something going wrong in the factory or from an inherent failure in the design. A drive shaft may vibrate too much because of a misaligned lathe or a misconceived shape; a motor may prove too hot because it was put together improperly or yanked into the design impetuously. The factor that brings this to a success is known as zero defects a form of quality control required during faulty assembly. There are symmetries between design for robustness and design for manufacturing. It has to be believed how robust products have become since the introduction of molded plastics and solid state circuitry. Instead of serving up many interconnected wires and tubes and switches—any one of which can fail-engineers can now imprint a million transistors on a virtually indestructible chip. In the modern world parts can be consolidated into subassemblies and mount them on molded frames that snap together. The principle for robustness are often indistinguishable from the principles of designing for manufacture—reduce the number of parts, consolidate subsystems, integrate the electronics. A robust product can tolerate greater variations in the production system. Please the customer and you will please the manufacturing manager. After preparing the variances in the field variations on the shop floor can be reduced. Manufacturing managers should stop trying to reduce process variations or to achieve the same variations with faster, cheaper processes. There are exceptions like in chip production where factory controls are even more stringent—although it is hard to think of exceptions like cars and consumer electronics. The factory is where workers meet and not deviate from the nominal targets set for products. Just like a product the factory may be said to give off an implicit signal—the consistent production of robust products-and to be subject of the disruptions of noise-variable temperatures, degraded machines, dust and so forth. Choices of the factory, like choices for the product, can be reduced to the cost of deviation from targets. A cylindrical grinder creates a cylindrical lathe more consistently than a lathe. Product designers have argued for such a dedicated machine, they want the greatest possible precision. Manufacturing engineers have traditionally favored the less precise lathe because it is more flexible and it reduces production cost.

In continuous flows the production process is dedicated to one or a few similar products. Production is continuous and level so that the lead time for production is uniform and predictable. Some examples are assembly lines, transfer lines and dedicated flow lines. Since production rates are uniform and predictable, material can be delivered to the process in a JIT manner. Work orders are not required since production is level. If the production mix is changed, the rates may be changed, but these changes are infrequent. In a batch or repetitive process parts of the process may resemble a continuous flow system while others involve multiple products produced in batches. Lead times are constant and predictable. The product mix is relatively constant but may have variations from month on month. Typical is production of parts and components for a high-volume end product-such as cars or electronics. Some parts and materials that are used uniformly can be delivered in a JIT manner. MRP is required to plan purchasing, delivery and co-ordination between plants. Similarly in a batch or dynamic processes, production is in batches, and the output mix and volume can vary, many customers come in with their orders on a weekly and monthly basis. As production mix and volumes change, many different materials and parts are required, departments must co-ordinate production. MRP must co-ordinate parts fabrication and assembly. Output varies too much for pull systems to work well. MRP does all the book-keeping on quantities, inventory availability and requirements, net of inventories. In custom engineering with low volume or complex engineered products or with custom manufacturing, there is no regularity in production patterns. MRP is invaluable only as an information management tool. It books orders, maintains bills, whether custom and standard and co-ordinates customer orders, shop orders and purchasing orders.

Manufacturers and retailers can alike greatly reduce the cost of forecasting errors by embracing accurate response, a new approach to entire forecasting planning and production process. Companies can redesign their planning process to minimize the result of inaccurate forecasts. Accurate response entails figuring out what forecasters can and cannot predict well and then make the supply chain fast and flexible so that managers can postpone decisions about unpredictable items until they have some market signals, such as early season sales results to match supply with demand. This approach takes into account missed sales opportunities that other forecasting techniques totally lack. Forecasting errors result in too much or too less inventory. Accurate forecasts also differentiates products of predictable demand to products of unpredictable demand. With these ideas not only do they rethink and overhaul all aspects of the supply chain—including the configuration of the supplier network, schedules for producing and delivering unfinished materials, transportation, and the number and location of warehouses but also the designs of their products. Any manufacturer whose capacity is constrained during peak production periods can make better use by making use of their off-peak capacity.

The tightness of the procedures that governs automated machine operation magnifies the harmful effects that faulty upstream processes have on downstream processes. Without machine operators physically handling parts, there is no one to realign them in a fixture, tweak cutting tools or compensate for small machining or operational errors, and nobody to inspect parts for holes, cracks, or other material defects. To replicate a machinist's talent for recognizing errors, engineers and supervisors of an automated system need either an elaborate data base incorporating, an expert system incorporating the implicit rules of the skilled machinist or a scientific understanding of the technology itself. Process engineers can provide the system sensors to detect errors and programmed controllers to interpret the sensors signals and initiate corrective actions or shut down the machines. Indeed production control data will increasingly become useless to human operators in real time as batches of materials move down the line. It is the computer that analyzes the microstructure of processing from one microsecond to the next and that takes the action against a badly made part. The manager's job is mainly taken up with making pieces fit together, both the equipment hardware and the programmed software. Men prepare to think more like computer programmers-people who break down production into a sequence of micro-steps. New hardware encourages more information sharing across the company, it enables different part of the manufacturing organization to become independent of one another. The new hardware encourages factories to break up into smaller units—plant—with—the—plant-of cells dedicated to making families of products. These mini-factories tend to be tightly integrated, organizationally flat, almost entirely self-managing and highly responsive to evolving market needs. The net result is reduced labor, reduced overhead, and increasing capacity utilization. The factory that emerges from such changes is likely to be smaller-between a third and a fifth of the size of traditional factories that generate similar volumes of products.

Incidentally the new technology can be a revolution between company and customer or between OEM suppliers and procurement officers. Mass production on the other hand shifted the emphasis of commerce away from service; Products had to designed to meet the needs of large markets. With mass production, the designer, producer and salesperson becomes three different people belonging to different parts of the organization. The new manufacturing technologies shift the focus from product features back to service, to customers. They also re-established close ties between producers and suppliers. CAD and CAE allow small organizations to design prototypes faster and more economically than before. Components can be produced efficiently in relatively small batches, essentially to order, through CAM and FMS.

Unfortunately most companies regard a manufacturing equipment choice as non strategic even though it may change the company's cost structure, improve its ability to introduce new products, and affect the way it interacts with its customers. Too often the operation of new manufacturing equipment is delegated to specialists, and equipment performance is tracked through the standard staffing, utilization and downtime reports. New equipment has little impact on how engineers design new products, how people are trained or how controllers monitor the manufacturing organization's performance. Integrated systems helps in calculating monthly shipments, redundant orders, redundant transaction processing and general confusion. Another type of data integration unites manufacturing databases to other functional areas. One company is integrating its complex multi-plant network with order entry and customer service network as to reduce overhead costs, increase delivery speed and effectiveness and improve the accuracy of its order entry. Advocates to manufacturing strategy and lean production consider the idea of focus differently based on products, processes or regions. Similarly high precision assembly may over time become routine for one plant but still be considered very difficult for a less experienced plant. As an organization gains operating experience difficult tasks become routine and it can take on additional complexity with little performance penalty.

Materials planning methods are the most adequate strategy for restructuring the materials process adequately. The first is known as a two bin system that are used as the controlling mechanism for very low value and very high usage consumable items, such as fasteners for which the cost of record keeping outweighs the benefits of inventory management. In an order-point system, stock replenishment is triggered by stock falling below a re-order point, which is calculated based upon the expected demand over the replenishment lead time. A safety stock is added, which is intended to give protection against the variability in the demand pattern. MRP is the process by which component parts are resources are planned to be manufactured or purchased and delivered, to satisfy the known or forecast demand, so that material shortages are eliminated and excess stocks are allowed to build up. MRPII can be summed up as respecting order priorities and delivery promises, Providing decision support for capacity planning, scheduling the flow of materials, ensuring the accuracy of the database via the closed loops, supporting differing planning horizons within a complex manufacturing environment. In developing a manufacturing strategy at first it is impossible to identify the key criteria that will determine whether or not a company occupies a competitive market position. These may differ depending on specific product/markets. It is important to assess how well or how badly the company's actual performance matches these criteria. It is important to satisfy the criteria of competitiveness and to focus on areas related to performance. Companies that have a profitable source of help at this stage, or the required competitive manufacturing strategies are competing in sufficiently removed geographical markets, companies utilizing a similar process technology but competing in different markets. It is important to redesign product structures so that individually customized product specifications are replaced by semi-standard products with customized features that will make demand more forecastable and therefore more stable. Reducing the lead time will do more than anything to eliminate conflict. As lead times decrease the operations flexibility increases.

From MRP comes MRPII. MRPII software forms the additional system integration: an interface is developed between a sales order processing module and the MPS module. The generation of sales analyses from the database generated by the sales order processing module, and the linking of the sales analysis data into a demand forecasting module. The linking of the forecasts generated into the MPS module to help drive the master schedule. Moreover the generation of actual or standard costs, and linking these into the financial systems. The MRPII software package also provides some degree of systems integration like: an interface between a CAD system and the bill of materials module, and EDI module, enabling translation of data into or from the protocol of an EDI network within the company's supply chain. A distribution resource planning sub-system DRP sub-system, can link to a downstream integrated distribution network with the overall MRPII planning system. There are many functional levels of MRPII: the presence or absence of system modules at the highest level of tactical planning, namely forecasting, and longer term production planning and resource planning. The presence or absence of business planning support tools, based on 4th generation language (4GL) software accessing the MRPII database, to assist business managers in strategic planning or highest-level tactical planning. The DRP or distribution resource planning modules act as a system server where end product inventories are wholly or partly held downstream in an integrated physical distribution system. The MRPII system module also shows a degree of interaction between the MPS and rough cut capacity planning modules. Non-standard solutions cater for make to order and jobbing shop environments, in which detailed production scheduling takes place that may in its turn drive materials requirement planning. Some systems may contain simple algorithms for smoothing production plans at the master production scheduling level. The system in this case recommends planned orders, using variations in planned inventory to achieve a level set of planned orders. This is most common in systems that cater to rate based scheduling or for a seasonal pattern of demand, where company policy may be to spread production evenly over a year and to build up inventory in advance of seasonal peaks. In this case it is important to recognize the planned inventory build up as a form of safety stock and to exclude it from available to promise calculation. The repetitive manufacturing module of the MRPII system may generate a final assembly schedule to match the predetermined rate of production by extracting orders from the sales order database in a specified order priority sequence.

Product development should be taken up as an important case of manufacturing strategy where to succeed, firms must be responsive to changing customer demands and moves of their competitors. This means that they must be fast. The ability to identify opportunities, mount the requisite development effort and bring to market new products and processes quickly which is critical to effective competition. But firms also must bring new products and processes to market efficiently. Because the number of new products and new process technologies has increased while model lives and life cycles have shrunk, firms must mount more development projects than has traditionally been the case utilizing substantially fewer resources per project. In the development imperatives required capability is fast and responsive that accelerates technological change and have shorter development cycles and better targeted products. Another important required capability is known as high development productivity, that explodes product variety, sophisticated discerning customers and has technical diversity that drives forward leverage from critical resources; and implies on increased number of successful development projects per engineer. The development imperatives consists of products with distinction and integrity that demands customers, crowded markets and intense competition and can drive forward creativity combined with total product quality and customers integrated with truly cross-functional developmental process. An obstacle to achieving rapid, efficient, high-quality development is the complexity and uncertainty that confronts engineers, marketers and manufacturers. A new design requires the development of new tools and equipment and uses the skills and capability of operators and technicians in the manufacturing plant. Of course, new products often require new skills and capabilities, but whether relying on new or old the success of the new product depends in part on how well it fits with the operating units and their chosen capabilities. However a firm may also choose to price its product to create superior value for its customers, thereby translating advantage in design and performance into increases in market share. Where lower costs are driven by growth and increases in volume, increases in market share may translate into improved position for the fast-cycle operator. Even if two competitors operate on the same learning curve, the fast cycle competitor will achieve a cost advantage. Speed in development is rooted in the ability to solve problems quickly and to integrate insight and understanding from engineering with critical pieces of knowledge in manufacturing. This set of capabilities likewise is critical in achieving cost reductions in established products. When costs are sensitive to volume and fast cycle-capability enhances a firm's overall learning capacity, the fast-cycle competitor enjoys double leverage in improving its manufacturing costs.

In the steel industry for example: a firm may seek to build an advantage in the quality and speed of its continuous casting operations. This is a technology based on sciences of metallurgy, thermodynamics, mechanics and electronic control; it requires know-how in machine design, computer modeling, materials development, metallurgy and electrical engineering. The steel firm engaged in continuous casting might engage in significant internal development—building experimental machines, developing prototype control systems-but also might enter into a partnership with equipment suppliers in the development of advanced controls and fund university research on heat transfer modeling. Managing the development of new products that is surrounded by investigations and shipping products, for this an organization should expand its knowledge base and have access to information in order to increase the number of new product and new process ideas. The second challenge is to narrow the funnel's neck. After generating a variety of alternating concepts and ideas, management must screen them and focus resources on the most attractive opportunities. Narrowing the funnel means the number of good projects that flow in.

The R&D group has to generate ideas for technologies and for new products and processes. They anticipate and encourage engineers and scientists to generate and explore many more ideas that will be applied in products and processes. A series of screens may be used—often involving peer reviews-to generate a winnowed down and manageable set of products and processes for market introduction. Early screens tend to be primarily technical in nature, focusing on technical feasibility and proof of concept. Later screens then shift to emphasize manufacturing feasibility and fundamental economics. As commercial introduction draws near, screens include added consideration of specific customer preferences, distribution channel concerns and financial return expectations. When project becomes successful, it often picks up ideas from competing projects that have lost momentum or has been screened out. Many times, however, even a project that passes through the funnel successfully and is introduced in the marketplace finds itself competing with other products offered by the firm. Thus to be successful over the long term, the resulting product must continue to compete successfully for sales, service and customer attention, not just against products from competitors, but against products from within the firm. Few products rarely become successful products. This is due first to the fact that carrying an idea all the way from research through to market introduction is an extremely expensive proposition, telling that research can generate too many ideas to be supported by the firm. In small firms for example in those manufacturing computer peripherals they repeat their success to subsequent generation of products after going through their challenges. If the mouth of the funnel is widened and is of three phases like: product or process idea generation and concept development, detailing of proposed project bounds and required knowledge and rapid focused development projects of multiple types. Ideas can be gathered from a variety of sources rather than R&D. One means for enlarging the mouth of the funnel is to institute procedures and incentives that encourage innovation and input from all parts of the organization as well as from customers, competitors and suppliers. Medical Electronics Inc developed a framework that also shows the abilities and problems like time is of the essence, engineers need to work new features and bring new technology into a coherent, integrated system, and where the product functions in a complex customer environment. All of this argues for a development framework that brings a broad, system perspective to the process and facilitates cross-functional integration. The MEI characteristics and issues in order are: at a reactive process as ad hoc sequence of actions stops and starts it faces problems of achieving focus, direction, and definition without missing opportunities and styling creativity. In a project organization where the characteristics are engineering focus; part-time job shop; frequent movement of people or prototype /testing where the characteristics are narrow focus on functional problems and sequential problem solving the main problems faced together in both the cases might be creating ownership and commitment to team; achieving continuity in the face of promotion and staffing needs; business as opposed to functional team or looking towards the issues of prototype/testing where the issues may be achieving integrated problem solving; using prototyping cycles to surface broader issues that cut across disciplines. Another motive may be to look at the real time adjustments that has characteristics of narrow focus on immediate problems; incomplete communication; problems handled through ad hoc changes of normal process and the issues can be creating discipline; capability for early resolution of conflicts; low-level rapid problem solving.

From engineering one needs good designs, well executed tests and high quality prototypes; from marketing one needs, thoughtful product positioning, solid customer analysis and well thought out product plans; from manufacturing one needs, capable processes, precise cost estimates, and skillful pilot production and ramp up. The MEI 2010 began as a concept and was defined during concept development through interactions between design engineering and marketing. In order for the corporation to approve investment in the project, marketing and engineering combined to give definition to the concept, apply estimates of cost and investment, and develop projections of likely volumes, revenues and profits. Approval by senior management triggered the design, construction, and testing of prototypes, as well as interaction with customers, as the organization moved to put ideas and concepts into practice. Once an engineering prototype was completed and verified, manufacturing moved in through the production prototype phase to define the process and develop the manufacturing system to be used in commercial production. This required identification of the process steps and their sequence, development of a bill of materials, selection of vendors and ordering of tooling. The production prototype phase culminated in the production of a small batch of the 2010 product. With pilot units in hand, quality assurance took the proposed product into customer tests while engineering handled redesign work that followed testing and customers reaction to the product. As testing moved forward, manufacturing prepared to ramp up for volume production while marketing trained the sales force and developed promotional programs. Once the product was launched into the market, field service supported customers in the use of the product. When the MEI engineering organization set out to develop an infant heart monitor, the challenge was to take existing core concepts and technology and develop and package them in a new, smaller, lightweight, portable design. The product as it emerged, was a design of a much smaller package and lower weight, but with many more features requiring new components, tighter tolerances and more capable manufacturing processes. Though the design was built on the core technology and was eventually manufactured in an existing plant, manufacturing had to do a significant amount of process development in order to create the required design capabilities. Manufacturing focused on the design and development of the process, including the flow of materials, the sequence of processing steps and the development of tools, after the engineers had established the product's basic architecture and implemented the architecture in hardware and software. Achieving an integrated product and process design require a very different approach. The focus of such an approach is to bring design choices into contact with process capabilities, and process capabilities into contact with design requirements early enough in the process. In an integrated process, the solution the solution to the vendor selection problem is apparent. The type of vendor to be used can be examined as design needs and requirements emerged.

Once the designer has framed the problem, the nest step in the design phase is to generate alternatives. Based on the developer's understanding of the relationship between design parameters and customer attributes, several alternative designs for physical models may be appropriate. The purpose of the alternative designs may be to explore the relationship between design parameters and specific customer attributes. If the particular design cycle under discussion comes at a later stage of the development, the purpose of the alternative designs may be to refine an established concept. In the second or build phase of the problem solving cycle, the developer builds working models of the design alternatives. The purpose of the second phase is to put alternative designs into a form that allows for testing. At an early stage of gear development, a developer may implement alternatives electronically in a computer aided design CAD workstation, using the computer to display graphically and visually the gears characteristics. In the build phase alternatives are created of which one it is easy to work with plastic or soft metals. In the third or test phase of the problem solving cycle, working models, prototypes or computer generated images are tested. In this design-build-test-cycle in the case of a gear noise, an early testing scheme may examine the decibel level generated by alternative designs. Subsequently given designs may be implemented with prototype parts and tested with prototype customers. In a laboratory setting, test engineers worry about things such as accuracy, precision, and the ability to calibrate measurements. Tests are subject to noise, or random variations caused by fluctuations in the environment that have not been accounted for or controlled. In order to cope with noise from, vibration, temperature, humidity, and even stray magnetic fields, engineers repeat tests several times to identify the amount of noise in the testing process. A single design-test-build cycle generates insight and information about the connection between specific design parameters and customer attributes. Thus the effectiveness of problem solving in development depends not only on the speed, productivity, quality of each individual step in the cycle, but also on the number of cycles required to achieve a solution. Much of this these days can be done in computers too. The fourth generation system takes integration across product and process design and marketing. The fourth-generation system may use a network diagram to structure the relationship between design parameters and customer attributes. The fourth generation system generates a more complex and electronic format for the kind of structured methodology like QFD and DFM. The fourth-generation system shortens feedback loop drastically, makes access to data more easier and more consistent and enhances the ability to communicate and collaborate. It generates organizational learning where due to appending notes, comments and test results the design team can communicate and manage complex data.

The purpose of prototyping is to demonstrate to the organization that the design has outstanding quality and high levels of manufacturability. Each prototyping cycle indicates how far development has progressed toward this goal and what is still required to reach it. The development cycles progress from architecture or product concept, through sub-system and system evaluation and verification, on the pilot production system verification, and eventually to production start-up. The evolution is from basic product concept, its aesthetics and shape, through the design engineering of specifications that provide product functionality. Much of the product design is verified as a total system, following which attention and responsibility shifts toward the production system that would build the car and eventually to the factory floor where volume production would take place. Since different prototype cycles have different purposes, different functions traditionally have taken responsibility of each one: early cycles have been the responsibility and domain of industrial designers and body engineers; middle cycles, the responsibility of various subsystem quality assurance engineers; and final cycles, the responsibility of manufacturing process engineers and factory operations. The cost and time to create prototypes shifts as well along with the locus of responsibility for various prototype cycles. After developing the CAD models, it is then followed by engineering built sub-system and system prototypes. Initial concept development ends when a simulated model or breadboard model or simulated version demonstrates feasibility of the basic product and its core concepts. Design maturity ends when the prototype from that phase works reliably under stress and conditions beginning to approach those representative of the customer's environment. Much like the sequence of prototype test cycles in automotive development project, workstation firms generally shift primary responsibility and involvement from engineering to manufacturing as the project progresses. When a technical breakthrough has a rapid response to engineering it gives creative, innovative results, manufacturing in late performance and features and easily overcome problems with manufacturing. Through a technical breakthrough it creates a system focus that causes technical compromise, complexity and uncertainty that slow down technical work and constraints of system that limit innovation. Technical breakthrough can replicate manufacturing early by slow turnarounds and late introductions, engineers out of loop and bringing late engineering changes. In an audit system few things can be defined like in the test and prototype system all mechanical systems will be piloted before commercial release, introduce new method for evaluating the tradeoffs between new and carry over parts, establish clear design-build-test cycles for prototyping, develop a test strategy that covers components, systems and subsystems and solve problems early. Real time adjustments can regenerate activity network after major changes, uses PERT system linked to formal development stages, establish a process for responding to new developments, compare planned schedule against tasks remaining and fix problems before moving forward.

Firms that succeed in building capability do so by finding a starting point-some aspects of the pattern of development through which to introduce change into the organization. Refining and upgrading what is fundamentally a sound approach is the appropriate starting point. There are 4 approaches to building a development capability. In the examples the interaction of approach and the firm's situation is illustrated, and the challenges involved in each approach and provide the context for identifying the common themes that characterize the strategies for change. The position of Physio Control that had a strong market position in emergency unit defribrillators and emergency unit heart monitors came under attack from aggressive small competitors who took advantage of regulatory and technology changes to open new product niches. Parts were designed by creating a series of objects such as points, lines, surfaces and dimensions that described the part. Objects could be grouped logically in a layer, and layers could be worked on individually or overlaid to generate a single part, a subassembly or an entire camera. It also facilitated the organization of control and change responsibility, with each layer being assigned to a single engineer who had control of change authorization. At the end it is important to pursue a demonstration project and create a development strategy by well-defined technical or market opportunity or demand for significant development improvement for project success and complex, changing product line; many project opportunities and increase in development requirements in the face of resource constraints.

Evaluating quality is another form of manufacturing strategy where the technical features can be listed that can meet customer requirements. These technical features are design attributes expressed in the technical language of the designer or engineer. They form the basis of subsequent design, manufacturing and service process activities. They can relate to customer attributes in a variety of ways. An improper relationship between customer attribute and technical feature suggest that either they are not being addressed and final product will have difficulty meeting customer needs or more market research is necessary. The evaluation of the technical features of competitive products can be produced. This is accomplished through in-house testing and translated into measurable terms. These evaluations are compared with competitive evaluation of customer attributes to detect inconsistencies. Targets for each technical feature are determined on the basis of customer existence ratings and existing product strengths and weaknesses. In the house of quality the main idea is selecting technical features to be deployed in the remainder of the process. Poor customer competitive performance or strong selling points have relationship with customer needs. These characteristics in turn have to be translated in the design and production process, so that proper actions and controls are taken to the voice of the customer. In the house of attributes QFD provide deployment matrix and control charts that provides the linkage of critical indicators for measurement, monitoring and improvement of the business process system to achieve customer satisfaction.

Chapter 4

Production analysis, synthesis and project management

(By Baisham Chatterjee)

In the case of production and production system a unit of output normally requires several types of inputs. In an industrial process it accounts for most of the variable cost of production. Conversion facilities are associated with fixed cost and the output produces the revenue. Elementary accounting declares that profit depends on the relationship of fixed and variable cost to revenue—the interaction of input and conversion costs to output revenue. Profit is a less apparent consideration in many service and government organizations, but these organizations still depend on balanced budgets and continued operation. As services such as healthcare have grown and government activities have proliferated in recent years, more attention is focused on the ratio of operating costs to the benefits for consumers. Efforts to reduce inputs and conversion costs, while maintaining or increasing output values, are using methods formerly associated with industrial production. Planning, analysis and control are more descriptive of the mental set of decision maker than a rigid problem solving procedure. Each phase is distinguished by an objective-to anticipate, to investigate, to regulate, to design. An evaluation of the existing system might have the objective of reducing costs and would likely begin with analysis of current operations and procedures. The results of the analysis phase could lead to planned improvements for which the collected data would fuel planning and control efforts.

Consumption is a multistage process. Relatively few producers deal with the consumer who is satisfying his or her personal wants. Most producers produce for other producers. Chain reaction effects can result from a switch in the consumer's wants. There are time lags of varying lengths throughout the production-to-consumption process. Largely unavoidable delays in gearing up to produce, and sluggish changes in market demands act as buffers to provide stability for production systems. Seldom do consumers all stop buying at once except in localized situations. Unless the whole economy is suffering, a switch from one type of consumption to another usually creates a shortage in the newly favored area that causes consumers to use the old products or services until new production capacity is ready. Consumer services in the public sector requires substantial time to start up, and old projects may wither but tend to linger interminably. The product/ service cycle warns that production systems must be dynamic in order to survive. A static system may appear during its zenith to be durable. This complacent view is seldom justified. Even when activities appear healthy and vigorous, planning should be underway to identify modifications that can improve operations and contingency plans should be constructed for major changes if internal and external conditions suddenly deteriorate. Thus each phase is subjected to planning analysis and control. To look at creating a better technological innovation environment in the modern world, every business should use the public who recognize the need to combat pollution, secure more sources of energy, expand mass-transit systems, find safer working conditions and cure for health hazards and attain other social goals. Some of these objectives can be made by refining discoveries made previously, but others depend on breakthrough that are still hidden from researchers. The search for discoveries is a very uncertain process, and the lag time between discovery and application is often discouragingly long. Where R&D fits into the organizational structure of a firm varies widely. It may be centralized to serve the entire corporation or be divided according to the firm's departments. A central research facility is easier to administer, but difficulties may arise in communicating problems between researchers and operating personnel. R&D is more closely linked to production when work is performed under manufacturing or when R&D is given a departmental status akin to manufacturing. Wider company participation in R&D can be obtained through an organizational approach known as project management. In this arrangement, selected people from different units in a firm are brought together to work as a team under a project manager. For the duration of the project, the manager has authority over the team members, budget and resources. The organizational structure associated with project management is called a matrix organization.

Production organizations are designed to generate an output. If the output is service, resources must be available to combine with professional skills to yield the desired service. Most functional divisions of an organization exhibit the following characteristics: regardless of the division of functional areas they overlap. Overlapping areas often require special attention and usually provide high returns for control effort. Links between functional areas form a communication network by which activities of an organization are coordinated. The less obvious functions are support functions and implied coordination of operations where: the indicated information and progress report paths illustrate only formal, usually preprinted, forms of paper flow communication. If all information channels were shown the diagram would resemble a windblown spider web. One half of the cycle is complete before material begins to flow physically in the production process. The period that must be allowed before the production actually begins is a prime consideration in planning. Each function is owed its share of lead time to prepare for a new product, order or style. Organizational sub-optimization is logically attacked by improving communications. The approach is far easier to recognize than it is to implement. Decisions are made on one level subject to review by an upper level and carried out by a lower level. Years of operation have proved that this orthogonal arrangement works. Modifications such as internal information centers are designed to take advantage of new high speed data processing machines. The advent of computers and automated data processing has certainly increased the timeliness, quantity, and quality of information, but it has not necessarily solved the problem of sub-optimization. In theory organizations flow of information and decisions concerning a tactical portion of the production system, such a flow should make each production decision compatible with the total organization policy. Some companies grow by adding new but related products to their basic line. As the technology increases, a company has to run to just maintain its present position. Each new advance means at least a model change to remain competitive. Each model change means a wider range of products because some users stay loyal to older, familiar models. Product and production planning must organize or even govern the explosion of catalog offering. Insular sub-optimization deals with a tendency to focus on the solution to a particular issue at the suspense of wider welfare. One product in a family of related products could be in trouble. To extract this product from its unfavorable position, it is necessary to redeploy company resources such as advertising budgets, engineering time, and capital investments.

The planning phase for a product starts with research to determine roughly its acceptability. If the concept appears promising, R&D efforts, as described are accelerated and market research efforts are launched to verify the potential demand. As the basic design becomes firm and production facilities are developed, the first promotion activities commence. Successful markets ensure that units will be sold at a minimum lag time from their production schedule. Production costs precede revenue from sales, so that financial consideration pressure managers to have sales dollars flowing in as soon as possible to recover the invested capital. Production costs level off after an initial peak caused by start-up expenses. Marketing costs usually decline after initial advertising and promotion expenses, and the R&D costs almost cease as attention is diverted from the original products to other products. A saturation point is reached at which sales decline because of a diminishing number of potential customers who remain unaware of the product, the replacement demand subsides and better products or substitutes enter the market. A refined model may be a major revision or merely a face-lift of the original. In either situation some R&D costs are incurred, and an upsurge in marketing cost is required to promote the new model. Production cost increases again to accommodate the changes needed to produce the modified output. If the renewal is successful, the product builds on its past record to achieve new sales records. Capacity planning attempts to integrate the factors of production so as to minimize facility costs over the life of a product or project. Because there are a bewildering number of individual facility designs involved in introducing a major new product, an early planning step is to determine a realistic sales goal. The total number should be large enough to recover investment yet be well within the market potential.

The distribution method is more versatile than the graphical routine and retains the succinctness that makes it a worthy tool for manual calculation. It is used to determine the preferred routes for the transportation of supplies from a number of origins of different destinations. Although the name distribution tends to conjure up images of warehouses supplying retail outlets with produce, the method also can be used to identify least cost or most profitable distribution pattern for any resource. The solution format defines: the amount and location of both supply and demand, the cost or profit created by supplying one unit from every origin to every destination. There is no limit to the number of origins or destinations that can be included in the matrix. An optimal distribution is obtained by first developing an initial solution and then sequentially testing and revising improved solutions until no further improvements are available. There may be several equal cost distribution patterns. Solution procedures identify the alternative routes. The companies in metropolitan centers which provide products to adjacent smaller communities and these plants operate at full capacity but cannot meet current demand. Unless expected competition appears, the market potential should continue to grow. To meet the anticipated demand a new plant is created in one of the two locations being served. The additional capacity will satisfy the local sales of the city in which the plant is located and the demand of the nearby cities. Rectangles represent plant-distribution centers and circles represent the outlying cities where the products are sold. They provide a rough indication of capacity. The arcs show possible distribution patterns. During transportation the product mix of the goods is customized to market demand. The total contribution is a function of the mix, but the transportation cost is a function of the volume moved. Therefore supply, demand, and transportation costs are rated in units or truckloads.

Taking the case of aggregate planning, planning inputs is the internal idea which is the best idea to reduce costs. Demands for products or service are seldom constant over several months. A prerequisite to aggregate planning is the development of a forecast. The predictions typically concern the overall level of demand, not broken down to a specific mix within a product line. Planners need to know what options are available to meet demand variations and the costs of the options. Options vary due to different management policies. A policy might be to never run out of stock. A more lenient policy could be to allow a stock out occasionally while making sure that customers orders are filled within two weeks. The costs of the options are not always recorded in accounting standards. The purpose of the production plan is to smooth out or eliminate sporadic disruptions in operations caused by fluctuations in demands. This is accomplished by scheduling operations to meet demand patterns over several periods in the future. If demand for product declined for 6 months and then soared for 6 months. As the demand rose, the manager would likely hire, institute overtime or fall behind in meeting orders. These short-term reaction can hurt the morale of the work force, reduce productivity and increase personnel costs. Parametric production planning is another search routine. This model assumes two linear feedback rules, one for the work force and the section for the production rate. Then the relevant costs are developed from the actual costs of the organization being studied. A preferred solution is identified by applying a grid search technique. Both simulation and computer search models are especially promising for tailor-made applications to unusual or unwieldy aggregate planning situations. A few aggregate planning models include learning effects. It is not uncommon for productivity rates to increase as additional production experience is gained. Increases are quantitatively described by learning curves or manufacturing progress functions. A combination of productivity growth with aggregate planning recognizes situations that makes workers more proficient with practical experience and thereby change workforce and material requirements. A learning function is often used as a model that includes mathematical expressions to include direct labor, variable labor overhead, hiring and firing and inventory carrying and shortage costs. The direct labor term reflects productivity improvement as a function of the cumulative production output.

The initial step in a CPM application is to break the project down into its component operations to form a complete list of essential activities. This task may appear easy but is usually difficult. The burden is the importance of a representative list where all subsequent steps are meaningless. An activity is a time consuming task with a distinct beginning and end point. The start of the first activity could be signaled by the receipt of a specification listing from the customer and could end when detailed sketches are delivered to the drafting and order department. The activity list prerequisite—post requisite consists of

an extensive listing, such as all the jobs that follow each activity, is unnecessarily tedious and even contributes to errors. As much of the CPM language has been introduced already, the language can be transferred into graphical representation. An activity is represented by a line or arrow. They connect two events, each event is a specific point in time marking the beginning or end of an activity. When two or more activities end with the same event, the event, that event is referred to as merge. Similarly when two or more activities begin at the same time, the event denoting the time is called a burst. A dashed line arrow is used in a network to show the dependency of one activity on another. It is called a network dummy activity and has all the restrictive properties of regular activities except that it requires zero time. The employment of dummies can be distinguished according to the purpose they serve; an artificial dummy is inserted to facilitate node numbering for computer applications and a logic dummy is necessary to portray graphically certain restraint relationship between nodes. The visual representation of the CPM network is a noteworthy communication device. The relationship of each part of the whole project is easier to comprehend when it is in network form and mistakes of omissions are more apparent. Drawing techniques vary and the initial attempt to graph a project is usually an approximate sketch. The general flow is evaluated and after the overall sequence is checked the compound activities can be sub-divided into detailed operations. Large projects are handled by treating sub-divisions independently in preliminary networks and then integrating them into dummy arrows to relate the segment. Thus the network pictures how a project can be done, whereas a schedule establishes how it is planned to be done. Two approaches are available for estimating activity durations, a deterministic approach and a statistical approach. An initial network often reveals that a project will take longer than anticipated. The critical path exposes the group of activities from which cuts should be made to shorten the project, but it does not indicate which cuts will be least expensive. To obtain a cost priority for reducing the project duration, more information can be used if the boundary time calculations is needed. Manual methods are available for determining not only which activities should be cut to meet a deadline but also the least expensive project duration when both direct and indirect project costs are considered. The procedure is to identify an ascending order of activity-cutting costs and make time reductions by using the lowest cost available. Where CPM fits into production, production environments that are more conducive to network planning have the following characteristics where in the first case, products are complex and essentially one of a kind, yet several products are manufactured at the same time in one facility. Start dates and delivery schedules are difficult to predict. Design and manufacturing groups work as teams on each product/project. Manufacturing methods and tooling vary from one product to the next, sometimes requiring significant modifications or new developments.

In a facilities layout, plant layout is a companion problem to plant location. A decision to relocate provides an opportunity to improve total facilities and services. A decision not to relocate is often accomplished by plans to revise the current plant arrangement. The re-layout may be designed to reduce increasing production costs that gradually evolve from piecemeal expansion or to introduce a new process. The re-layout strives to maximize production flow and labor effectiveness. Facilities layout is to design a physical arrangement that most economically meets the required output quantity and quality. A fairly stable demand forecast allows the facility design to include refinements that would not be feasible for processes that are subject to rapid technological change or output sensitive to big swings in customer tastes. The general layout for product flow follows a pattern set by the type of production anticipated. A line or chain of facilities and auxiliary services through which a product is progressively refined is known as product layout. This layout is characteristic of mass or continuous production. A logical sequence of operations reduces material handling and inventories usually lowers the production cost per unit, and is easier to control and supervise. These advantages are achieved at the expense of flexibility. Any changes in the design and volume of the product normally require a major investment. On the other hand process layout is a grouping of machines and services according to common functions for the performance of distinct operations such as welding, painting, typing or shipping. Job and batch production allows good flexibility and reduces the investment in machines, but it also looks at handling, space requirement, production time and the need for close supervision and planning. Fixed position layout is an arrangement in which people and machines are brought to a product that is fixed in one position owing to its size. Shipbuilding and heavy construction of dams, bridges and buildings are typical examples. Such operations often enjoy high worker morale and flexibility for scheduling and design changes. Each layout has relative advantages. Sometimes the advantages characteristic of one type can be imposed on another type to produce a hybrid that lowers cost for special applications. Similarly the flexibility of a high-volume, high-investment production line is increased by planning foresight that provides space and hookups i.e power, waste disposal and material supply for future modifications. All sorts of product flow lines can be imagined—up or down, unidirectional or cross flow, centralized or decentralized. The problem is to determine which design from a multitude of possibilities best fits today's needs and is amenable to tomorrows potential. A product layout usually allows less discretion for arrangement because it depends mostly on the technology involved. It is a continuous line from raw material to finished product which is exemplified by large automobile assembly or food processing lines and by smaller labor intensive lines that fabricate special sub-assemblies. Over 3 million different patterns are available for a process layout composed of 10 departments, assuming there are no constraints. Architectural limitations, production requirements, safety rules probably complicate the safety rules. Parts and material flow has human as well as product advantages and disadvantages, like the economically recommended mass-production assembly line. Equipment and supplies used by workers should be designed and arranged for minimum effort and maximum convenience. For equipment design the key word is flexibility. Adjustable equipment avoids the need for individually fitted designs as well as substandard performance from workers. Supplies, materials and tools cannot always be placed within each reach of the worker, but they should be arranged as conveniently possible. Communication links determines the control relationship between workers and machines, communication links include visual and auditory from worker to worker or from equipment to worker. A link analysis is conducted by determining the types of links involved, assigning a value to each link, and then evaluating different arrangements of operators and machines with respect to links.

In the process analysis measurement includes both the determination of time standards for work as well as ideas like wage payments for the work done. Time study or setting a time for the specific task and work sampling are important applications for work and time measurement. Charting finds three systems in production studies: survey, design and presentation. Survey charts are used in the initial phase of an investigation to categorize present procedures. Design charts expose planned innovations to critical reviews which filter out the most promising designs. The first step in a process analysis is to decide which process to investigate. The process with better improvement promises the greatest return. Operating departments usually suggest areas when methods work in a staff function. Background information for setting priorities of studies is obtained by reviewing reports, memoranda and directives.

Machine tooling refers to the selection and design of cutting tools, jigs, dies required to perform a specific operation. Tool engineering has got a lot to do with operating efficiency of machines. A decision as to whether an air chuck or a mechanical chuck should be used; whether a cemented carbide tool or one made from high speed steel will perform better, which is a better coolant, what feeds and speeds produce the satisfactory results. In the industry in which change is rapid or unpredictable this loss of fluidity may be serious. During a business recession or when volume decreases, an automated line cannot be laid off or employed in other work. The downtime of the equipment is apt to be devilishly expensive. Assembly line balancing is associated with product layout where products are refined as they pass through a line of work centers. The period allowed to complete operations at each station is determined by speeds of assembly time and cycle time. Idle or float time is created for a station when the work assigned to it takes less time than does the set cycle time. Line balancing problems have received greater attention than assembly line warrants. Moreover the approach to line balancing is realized when the dynamic nature of the product line is considered. The sequence of operations seldom varies, but the operation times are far from constant. Fluctuating flow between stations means the operators must co-operate to balance internally one another's work output with the pace of the assembly line. Human behaviors might remain as an effective factor in effective line balancing. A provision for activating a stand-by machine when an on-line machine fails is another way to maintain service. A stand by machine must be periodically checked, takes space and depreciates in value whether or not it is used. The availability of a substitute to keep an operation line functioning can avert a slowdown or shutdown of a whole series of dependant operations.

There are many production control designs, which can be considered into three basic types that fit into situations. A control system designed for one plant might not work in another and might not even remain effective for the original plant as production requirements change. In continuous production there is usage of a product layout that creates standardized end product and manufacturing routine, high volume of output produced by specialized equipment and low in process inventory and long production runs. Even intermittent production uses a process layout with the nonstandard end product requiring extensive production control, medium volume of output produced by general purpose equipment, there is found to be high in-process inventory and shorter production runs and more flexible process owing to versatile material handling equipment. Flow or serialized control applies to control of continuous production as found in oil refineries, bottling works, cigarette making factories, papermaking mills and other mass manufacturing plants. The standardization of products, equipments and work assignments allows the controls to be standardized also. The high volume production means that huge quantities of raw materials must be accumulated and stored until needed. Because of the inflexibility of the process, the entire operation is curtailed by a shortage of material in any part of the sequence. The volume of output requires strict attention to the finished goods inventory and a smoothly operating distribution system.

Order control associated with intermittent production, is far more complex than is flow control. The job-shop nature of the work means that production orders may come from different sources and for different quantities and designs; the time allowed for production also may vary as a result of salespeople's delivery promises. These conditions make prior planning difficult and necessitate a high degree of control over each order. The bill of material: like name and model of product, order number and quantity, raw materials, parts by name and number and appropriate specifications, drawings and other references, routing information as to the sequence of operations, and desired delivery dates are considered in making the work schedule. The two principal methods of scheduling are backward scheduling to meet a deadline and forward scheduling to produce as soon as possible. When several subassemblies with different lead times are involved, the scheduler must work backward along each subassembly line to set the times for component work orders. Forward scheduling is used more frequently for products whose components do not require assembly. The scheduler issues orders to begin production as soon as the machine time is available. When there is a backlog of demand, the requested delivery date is checked to set priority; then the backward and forward scheduling is combined.

Product designers stand astride the quality demands of customers and the quality capabilities of producers. Their first responsibility is to design a product wanted by consumers. They are assisted by market research and other staff efforts. The product design must be set within the capabilities of producer and requisites of the buyer. The quality theme underscoring production activities is continuous control. Its manifestation take many forms and provoke diverse attitudes. Statistical formulas are very important and compatible to the production process with quality directives. Inspectors make measurements and observations to effectuate the statistical design. Supervisors are at the interface between the quality goals set by top management and the execution of programs to attain the goals, an important position in all quality control efforts. The cost of vigilance is primarily constituted by inspection, a seemingly contradictory inspection cost-value relationship as between the costs of vigilance and error that vary inversely. Higher inspection costs, if the money is wisely spent, will detect a greater proportion of defects and thereby provide a greater degree of protection from the effects of defective output. As the number of undetected defects decreases, a point is reached where further improvement is unnecessary because the higher quality does not proportionately increase the value of the product. In some processes the purpose of inspection is to examine all the output to discover any defective workmanship. For special projects such as construction work, a single item may be inspected several times during its development. In other processes inspection means inspecting samples from the total output. The statistical design plan of the sampling plan attempts to minimize the inspection cost while maintaining a desired level of confidence that the process is within established control limits.

Productivity—improvement effort is focused on the people who actually produce the output, by the direct measurement of their performance. Productivity indicators differ from the standards set for accomplishing a given amount of work within a given time. Team indicators measure the characteristic of an operation of project carried out by a group of people. The criterion for inclusion is that all members of the group are producing a definable end product of accomplishment—maintenance of production facilities, operation of a warehouse, administrative function like accounting, fabrication of a subassembly, the issuing of licenses and the completion of one stage of production.

In the production stage a set of objectives may be included in the system. The manager partitions his large system into subsystems, only partial effects on purposes are embodied in these subsystems. The character of sub-optimization is a result of detailed subsystem decisions only designed to optimize performance of subsystems. Models can be concrete such as architectural models of buildings, designer's prototypes of autos, charts, maps and blueprints or abstract such as organization charts and systems of mathematical equations. The total unification of the production management field would be achieved if the entire system of equations described the effect of all relevant factors of all system objectives. In the first examination of a break-even chart the assumption of linearity is not a major concession because linear relationships do adequately describe many situations. The second line reflects the variable cost components which increase with additional volume. The variable cost is added to the fixed cost which would exist in any case at a zero production level. Although not as quickly recognized, methodological change can produce the same kind of result as a technological breakthrough. Because of inventory theory, for example, the costs of operating a particular line of business may be altered substantially. Profit comparison might bring a change in global strategy. Global strategies tend to be more intensive to methodological advances than to technological ones. This may be inspired by a pre-conceived notion that only technological changes are of paramount importance. The development of high-speed electronic computers with a technological advance plus the creation of ingenious methods that are only feasible with computers is a good example of how closely related both kinds of change can be. A real decision system can contain more or less detail, but the theory is unchanged by detail. The decision level is important in practice and not significant to theory. The production manager must never lose sight of the fact that he is dealing with a total problem. He is working on a tactical level so that the local and global strategies are made. Short cycle decisions if repeated over and over again, can also result in ruin when the decision repeatedly imposes even a small penalty on the company. Rejects, customer returns, back orders, machine-idle times, set-up costs or absenteeism are increasing even before one-way doors are passed. Control can be exercised through design where there is culmination of technological knowledge and methodological analysis. The instruments are not always totally under control. The variability of instrument performance is what makes golf an interesting game, similarly the control over strategic resource is not always precise. This is characteristic of financial control. The production manager must deal with both physical and behavioral systems. Production management is involved with both determinate and non-determinate systems. Similarly as different parts of it, blueprints are a detailed description of output and explain what is to be done. The language of blueprints consists of conventions of spatial configuration and abstract written symbols as well. Non-fabricating systems have means of visual expression that are comparable. Both product and process blueprints must be drawn in total detail. This is an engineering job requiring highly specialized technological knowledge. The equivalent of the blueprint in service department is a carefully detailed statement of the systems output, that is, the service to be provided under all conditions that are likely to be experienced. According to project accomplishment per period of time the environmental and work force conditions remain relatively stable over each particular interval. Thus productivity per phase can be measured rather than in aggregate. An average measure of productivity can be obtained for the total project. The research task can be divided at least in theory in unit phases or accomplishment units. Group size for minimum cost is smaller than for minimum product development time and the optimal group size is dependant on the managers objectives. Product development moves through many phases where different functional areas of interest must be integrated and coordinated Inventory policy can affect delivery delays; national distribution of product usually requires extensive back-up stock and shelf movement will be affected by promotional and advertising timing.

When possible engineers transform the result obtained from experiments with scale models to overcome the inherent distortions on the prototypes. Differences in physical size must be properly rationalized as they affect performance. Scaled down energy inputs and outputs may not behave in linear proportion to the full scale system. Materials aging experiments require a reduction of time, as do most fatigue tests, but the effects of artificially compressing time must be completely understood if the prototype is to be used to predict the performance of the full-scale unit operating in real time. Even for styling and appearance, the scaled down prototype can mislead design judgment. Consequently the decision is made to test market the alternatives. It is difficult to design a test marketing situation that incorporates all the relevant features existing in the full-scale market. Using sampling theory and a great deal of statistical information, a reasonable approximation can be obtained. The products themselves might be prototypes if the production line cannot be set up until a decision is reached. Where there is high resource convertibility, the company's planning can be very flexible. Technological knowledge may be the least convertible resource to the production manager, but he is quite flexible with respect to the kind of technological system that might be managed. Operating within the accustomed framework of limited resources, a company must determine its optimal product or output mix. The optimal mix is defined as the mix of products and services, using the existing resources and facilities of the company, which will maximize profit.

From The fundamental theorem of linear programming it can be understood that the number of parts plus the number of any other resource constraints such as storage space, limited power, or scarce raw material will be equal to the maximum number of products that can be included in the ultimate composition of the product mix. A veritable revolution in design ability is required in order to move in the direction of interchangeable modules. The roots of such efforts already exist in the well developed concept of standard parts (e.g. screw thread gauges, and light bulbs) and in standard process operations(e.g, synthetic time, standards and computer controlled equipment). When referred to the fact that the functional attributes will continue to perform within some set of limits over a given period of time. The width of the limits represents an important aspect of the definition of quality for the design. A unit can have very erratic performance before it reaches the failure threshold, for example the light bulb might get alternately brighter and dimmer. This constitutes still another measure of reliability, that is the specification of allowable variability of performance. Reliability is not a simple dimension. Both reliability and failure can be described successfully only by using statistical terms because, it can be predicted how long the unit can be expected to continue to function satisfactorily. Quality is concerned with ease of maintenance and the cost of replacement parts. In search for greater control on quality a central materials control department appears in all organizations. Materials control has three sub-functions like procurement or purchasing, inventory control and acceptance sampling. Many forms of communication must flow between the organizational units in order to achieve an integrated materials control department. Materials control department communicates with the production division with other operating divisions of the company in many ways with the external world. Vendor relations depend to a great extent on the nature of a company's operations. Bypassing mail order, wholesale and retail inventories, purchase inventories can be divided into two major parts. Like materials required for production and materials required for maintenance of plant and equipment. Some companies purchase manufactured and assembled items; other companies deal primarily with basic raw materials and commodity markets.

 The purchase of fabricated units and components tends to involve more stable price structures than apply to commodity. An organization will contract with a producer to supply a given number of units of some specific quality. The contract may be given on the basis of bids which are offered by potential vendors. The economic lot-size model and the economic order-quantity model are based on the assumption that there will be no variability in demand. In true in sense in modern production era a lot of inventory models has been designed to cope with situations where the design level fluctuates. Many companies use perpetual inventory system wherein withdrawal quantities are entered on the item's stock card each and every time each and every time that a unit is withdrawn from stock. The withdrawal quantity is subtracted from the previous stock level to determine present quantity of stock on hand. A minimum level is designated as the reorder level for each item. When a minimum level is reached then an order is placed for the economic order quantity.

Flow charts can be exceedingly helpful for process development of analytic systems. In the automobile production line each component is brought in at the appropriate point after which it looses its separate identity. Most processes combine both analytic and synthetic operations. Labor costs are one of the most important factors in the determination of a suitable plant location for certain labor intensive industries. With increasing mechanization the labor problem has been alleviated to an extent for all industries. There has also been a reduction in differential wage rates by regions of the country. Different schedules will arise according to the nature of the costs. The plant location interacts specifically with many other production management problem. The size of the labor market and the attitudes of labor unions can figure heavily in the plant location decisions. Many processes require special environments. When the technology of the process require large amounts of water then only a location where such water resources are available can be considered. It is important to locate not so environment friendly plant in such a place where the pollution can be controlled. There is necessary of sufficient amount of power and look for creating or searching locations that can create a heavy demand. Frequently when a plant-rental arrangement is used, basic structural changes either are prohibited or are not economically sensible. When an existing structure has been purchased it may not be economically feasible to knock down walls, add sections and make other structural changes. The relative permanency desired for any physical arrangement of components is a matter that arises later. If a continuous production line is to be set up, it obviously presents different conditions than would be encountered in a job-shop system.

With increasing automation the importance of labor estimation problem is reduced. To achieve increased levels of certainty, the production manager exhibits a tendency to move towards automation. There has been growth rate in the wage rates of indirect, administrative, sales promotional and creative personnel. The problem of assigning such costs to the output has taken time to resolve. Uncertainties in consumer demand exact a greater toll when automated processes are utilized. Cost controls imposed by financial management once again started to exert their constriction. To control day to day operations the production manager had also to learn to cope with providing information to more sophisticated cost accounting and budgetary system. Recent technological developments have reduced the size of maximum production facility in a number of industries: return on capital investment does not increase commensurately from the smallest to the largest production facility. The increased precision of the inventory control enhances attention to the cost of extended delivery times and augments awareness for the cost of keeping goods in transit. All these take their process at times of project management. The first thing about project management is concept-where need for project evolves and gives importance to the organization to justify the diversion of resources from the normal day-to-day activities. The technical feasibility has to be checked and the time and cost involved and the resources required has to be looked at. The modern form of project initiation consists of: developing a new product, entering a new marketplace, installing a new computer system, selecting and installing a new process, retraining in new technologies and techniques, improving quality levels, reducing operating costs, refocusing managerial priorities, meeting new legislation, solving a major environmental problem and amalgamating with another organization. The four reframing ideas deal with operational capability, technical capability, time scale and disruptions. Internal skill and experience available to operate and maintain an alternative is the priority. It is important to understand the project teams technical competence to design and evaluate an alternative. The longer the timescale the lower the points gained. It is easier and better to have several limited connected projects than to try and have them rolled into one big project. Among the laws of project management it is said that no major project is ever installed on time, within budget and within the same staff that started it. Projects progress quickly until they are 90% complete. If project content is allowed to change freely the rate of change will exceed the rate of progress. Often projects have difficulty in staying within budget and still maintaining the schedule. Often projects have difficulty in delivering the full specifications within the scheduled time span which all together mean that it is uncertain how long an individual activity will take which often exceeds that estimated. Project summary shows overall start or finish information and variances of the overall projects such as dates, duration, work, cost and activity status.

The site acquisitions activity is critical for the follow-on planning permission activity and this needs checking to see why the finish date has slipped. If in the case of a project completion there is chance for the project date being delayed then the start dates of all other activities may have to be changed, or special changes will need to be made to some activities to catch up on the slippage to ensure that the overall completion date is held. When the design activity is behind schedule, it may be possible to switch staff to help some other activity, perhaps on a different project within the section. The main duty of the project manager is to take action, with the note of cost and time of present activity. Make an impact analysis which is required where the recovery cannot be achieved within the ongoing activity. This requires wide consultation with all concerned to reschedule if necessary the remainder of the project. This helps to resolve issues within sections and needs creativity in contingency usage, making available more resources, changing dates or reducing scope.

Chapter 5

Production focus and processes for development, the ideal economics, How it started?

(By BAISHAM CHATTERJEE)

The relationship between information and control systems brings into account a generalized production system. Inputs may be processed into any specified sequence of operations but may vary from one to any finite number. Whenever we talk of modern production aspects, we talk of continuous flow production situations where the facilities are standardized as to routings and flow since inputs are standardized. Therefore a standard set of processes and sequence of processes can be adopted. Continuous models are represented in practice by production and assembly lines, large scale office operations processing forms by standard procedure and continuous flow chemical operations. In intermittent production situations facilities must be flexible enough to handle a wide variety of products and sizes, or where the change in basic nature of the activity imposes change in product design. Transportation facilities between operations also must be flexible to accommodate a wide variety of input characteristics as well as a wide variety of routes that the inputs may require. Many diverse activities occur within the systems, regardless of their setting. The operations phase of activities is characterized by some input, processing or transformation and an output. In case of continuous flow production system, input-output characteristics are standardized, allowing standardization of operations and their sequence. Minor storage of inputs occurs after receipt. On the other hand, if the order is for goods, service or energy, which cannot be filled from inventory, it is routed to that function. When orders are sent to operations, the intelligence arm or professional and/or service function must satisfy operations with the necessary labor, materials, energy, equipment and external services all at the correct time and of the right kind. Thus information must be sent through the employment policy and the financial and ordering policy functions so that order may go out to the various pools and on receipt of the order the labor pool routes people into the system.

After the ordering policies are defined and scrutinized, when the system policies are defined the result is suboptimum solution. Sub-optimization occurs, if in attempting to determine a program for the production of a seasonal product, that establishes the scope of the problem as being one of the minimizing labor costs. The level production program is a suboptimum solution in this instance; a solution that considers both labor and inventory costs will specify a balance between these costs rather than minimizing either of them by ignoring the other. Other problems that need a solution are: costs of carrying inventory to absorb fluctuations in sales level.

Breakeven points helps in increasing profits and makes use of fixed and variable nature of costs to indicate the range of volume necessary for profitable operation. To increase plant capacity, factory fixed costs are increased. If the variable cost characteristics are the same as for existing plant and equipment, the breakeven point would go up. If we assume that sales volume can go up in proportion to the increased capacity, profit would go up more than proportionally. Often the new capacity has lower variable costs because of improved layout, labor-saving devices and other technological improvements. Similarly when obsolete plant or equipment are replaced, fixed costs will go up even though existing assets are disposed of. Development of new equipment with lower variable cost leads to obsolescence. If unused capacity can be put to work, the net effect is on variable cost which has a direct effect on the breakeven point that is a description of manufacture of components previously bought. If fixed costs go up due to new equipment purchased then the net effect on breakeven point and gross profit will depend on direction and magnitude of change of variable cost. Effect of purchase of components previously manufactured depends on the actual magnitude of costs that can be disposed of. Most of the fixed costs remains, but disposal of some assets will be possible. Variable costs could change in either direction; the net effect on factory breakeven points and gross profits may be either positive or negative, depending upon the relative magnitudes of the disposals and increased variable costs. In the decision to increase capacity, variable costs increase and as a result breakeven point goes up. In this relationship profit will depend upon the relationships of the beginning and ending slopes of the total cost line and the magnitude of the actual volume gain.

While talking about the production processes it covers the entire spectrum from the completely manual task, through man-machine systems to automated processes where labor is either indirect or of a vigilance nature. Manual tasks, usually in combination with mechanical aids still account for a large share of productive activity. Some production processes have a considerable technological base, like metal-working industries, wood-working industries, plastics and chemicals. In the breakdown of a transport airplane, showing the effect of design alternatives on various major components of cost. In this breakdown minimum material cost is a sub-component, other factors are material cost influenced by design. Equipment costs outside design control, relationship and modification of equipment according to customer surveys. Equipment costs influenced by design and minimum labor cost that is directly influenced by design are both essential components of direct labor. Similarly tooling and engineering have tooling and engineering costs involved. Process planning must begin during the design stages where selection of materials and initial forms, such as castings, forgings and die-castings take place. This is manifested by drawing release which summarizes the exact specification of what is to be made. Process planning necessarily blends with the layout of physical activities. Some process planning takes place during the layout phases of the design of a production system.

Assuming that the product is engineered, the complete drawings and specifications of the parts and their dimensions, tolerances and materials are to be used. Decisions have to be made as to which parts to purchase and which to manufacture in the plant. The engineering drawings specify the locations, sizes and tolerances for holes to be drilled, surfaces to be finished etc. After the engineering drawings and product verifications are specified we look at the cost aspects. People want to vary from the policy only in situations which they regard as limiting, such as when quality considerations, supply, patents, dictate a certain course of action. In reengineering nuts, bolts, switches and valves are often required, although recently many more complicated tools are also used. Although it may be a make-buy policy. It forms the entire plant load. It would be a common practice for which basic processes are already available, but if plant load requires overtime work, economic analysis may change considerably.

Buying of parts increases automatically, reflecting a recognition of the effect of overtime premiums, as well as the need to increase effective capacity to meet schedules.

PERT and CPM are other network planning methods, where PERT methods are based on probabilistic estimates of activity times which resulted in a probabilistic path through a network of activities and a probabilistic project completion time. The CPM assumed deterministic activity time and are defined through a probabilistic-deterministic arrow diagram. Arrow diagramming, activity analysis, dummy activities, node numbering are parts of PERT planning methods.

After the most important production activities are settled, we try to understand the dynamic nature of plant locations where instead of expanding physical activities, we expand subcontracting to achieve overall expansion. It is important to expand the existing plant if possible. Retain the existing plant and locate a second one elsewhere that can easily satisfy and correlate to the efficiencies of the products, logistics and supply chains and on demand activities. If till then it is difficult to correlate or satisfy the modern methods of doing business, then it is necessary to junk the old plant and relocate everything in the new one. Sometimes building a plant depends on current costs, demand breakdowns and an assessment of the future. If the balance of these factors changes then the capacity of markets should change in order to yield a minimum total cost for whatever conditions exist.

Plant layout is the integrating phase of the design of a production system. The basic objective of layout is to develop a production system that meets requirements of capacity and quality in the most economical way. Here the specifications of what to make, how it is to be made, and how many to make become the basis for developing an integrated system of production. The integrated system must provide for: machines, workplaces, and storage in the capacities required so that feasible schedules can be determined for the various parts and products; a transportation system which moves the parts and products through the system; and auxiliary services for production, such as tool cribs and maintenance shops, and for personnel such as medical facilities and cafeterias. The production machine must retain an appropriate degree of flexibility to provide for future changes in product designs, product volumes, and mixes and for advancing production technology. Certain financial and physical restrictions are a normal part of the layout problem. The physical restrictions may be due to: its size, shape, and orientation in relation to roads, railroads and utilities. There are many problems of layout which seem to interact. Providing flexibility affects the nature of processes and capacities which in turn interact with short and long run costs. Material transportation methods affect not only transportation costs but also the amount of handling at machines and workplaces. The physical arrangement and relative location of work centers are important in determining transportation costs and direct labor costs. Storage locations and capacities interact with transportation costs and delay times.

Layouts can be classified as process oriented or product oriented. In a process layout, equipment of the same functional type is grouped together, so there could be lathes together, inspection in one place, assembly in one place. They follow the model for intermittent production systems shows the typical arrangement of product or line layout, which follows the model for continuous production systems. The name product layout comes from the fact that the basic organization of the layout is dictated by the part or product. Equipment is arranged according to the sequence in which it is used for a given part or product, following the route sheet sequences. Process layout is often called functional or job-lot layout. It is employed when the same facilities must be used to fabricate and assemble a wide variety of parts or when part and product design are not stable. The requirements can be summarized as an adequate volume that makes possible reasonable equipment utilization. The ability for bringing out low-cost manufacture helps in building a reasonably stable demand for product, product standardization, part interchangeability and continuous supply of material. Reasonably good equipment utilization is associated with volume. Stable demand is required in terms of a minimum run which would at least cover the extra costs of tooling the line. Thus, stable demand is associated with product standardization. Engineering changes in product designs can be accommodated by product lines, but they cannot be too frequent. There should be an economical run to cover the costs of retooling and re-layout where design changes may be required. Similarly in the case of materials handling in process layout there is necessity of flexibility: flexibility of path and flexibility of size, weight and shape of load. Equipments that fit this requirement are mobile trucks, tractors and cranes. Providing easy operations is the best idea for preparing a process layout. It is a common event to find a material handling equipment idle, a considerable share of the time and at the same time to hear complaints that the material can never be moved when it is wanted. Demand for transportation service can be analyzed and a distribution of equal arrival rates or arrival times can be constructed.

Although standard sizes and types of conveying equipment are available commercially, they ordinarily require a considerable amount of special design work to fit them into an overall design of line layout. The best systems of internal transportation for lines integrate the functions of transportation with those of processing and storage, so it is not necessary to perform supplementary handling to and from the line. Many processes like painting and drying, assembly takes place when the material moves. Line layout design often makes it worthwhile to design special handling equipment that is integrated with the processing so completely that the entire line functions as a single integrated machine. The typical transfer machine is a series of processing operations tied together by an integrated handling system. Much of the actual material handling performed in industry occurs as a part of the productive operations, such as moving parts to and from machines. Through integrated handling systems designed, the other handling systems can be eliminated.

Layouts and models using two and three dimensional templates have a wide area of application in the development and planning of new facilities, as well as in the re-layout of existing facilities which is a continual process to accommodate changes in products, manufacturing methods and technology moreover visualizing the development of a complex machine is known as a manufacturing plant. The resulting layout expresses the designers specifications of the locations of all equipment, storage areas, aisle space, utilities etc and the relationship between machines and departments. In a layout two-dimensional templates with correct figures like shape of roof, design of bay, roof support and range in width of bays gives additional detail, showing the outline of the machine itself, with dotted lines indicating maximum table movements.

Everybody is well aware of job content and job methods and are clear of all that as a basics. Similarly there is a relationship of factors determining job content and job methods, where the job content consists of: drive to gain the advantages of division of labor, limitations specified by product designs and existing processes, limitations specified by production quotas, limitations specified by layouts and pacing effects of machines and conveyors. The most important idea to bring all of these to a success is limitations specified by the desire to make skill requirements uniform within jobs and following and creating drives to gain the advantages of work satisfaction through job enlargement. The job methods include physical and economic limitations and control of the working environment. Job methods can be improved by physiological data and psychological data. Arrangement should be made on the flow of work and study of the motions and time required. The last component of job method is fatigue and work schedules. Designing of tools and equipment is the most important method for motion economy and fatigue reduction. The hands should be relieved of all work that can be done more advantageously by a jig, a fixture or a foot operated device. Similarly two or more tools should be combined whenever possible and similarly while the manufacturing process is ongoing tools and materials should be prepositioned whenever possible. While using a computer program or a computer software ideas like using the capacities of each finger to distribute the work load has been the new transformation.

In this age of mechanization, in the most advanced state, it was difficult to tell which links in the giant machine were mechanized and which were human. As a matter of fact, the machine designers look at the overall problem as one of the simply employing machine links in the most economical way. The job enlargement plan and the expansion of the scope and responsibility of jobs resulted in a re-evaluation of jobs with increased wages to compensate for increased skills and responsibilities. Company records showed a substantial reduction in losses from defect and scrap. There is greater responsibility taken by the individual operator for the quality of his work. Job enlargement and the benefits of job enlargement during a five-year record of a chemical plant or the right job given to the right person in a distribution department is another symbol of performing through a broad spectrum in a maintenance department where everything comes together. The different job designs in different departments can be formed as: line job design where separately tasks are performed on rotated basis by workers. In this production method workers rotate among nine stations on belt conveyor performing minute specified operations at pace of conveyor. In the case of group job design the purpose is eliminating conveyor pacing effects and other conditions primarily the same where workers rotate among nine individual stations using batch method. The last among the experimental conditions is individual job design that give workers experience on experimental job design where assembly tasks are performed by workers. The individual job design brought significant improvements like increasing the quality efficiency, increasing the flexibility of the production process, deficiency of individuals in productivity and quality, reduced service function like material delivery and inspection.

Production standards provide data that are basic to many decision-making problems in production. The production standard is of critical importance because labor cost is a predominant factor, influencing many decisions that must be made. Decision to make or buy, to replace equipment or to select certain manufacturing processes require estimates of labor costs, as well as estimates of other costs. These decisions necessarily require an estimate of how much output can be expected per unit of time. Production standards also helps in showing the day-to-day operations of a plant like scheduling or loading machines. Labor cost, bid price that refers the expected costs like labor, material, overhead and profit are the most important components for measuring production standards. Finally production standards provide the basis of labor cost control. By measuring worker performance in comparison to standard performance, indexes can be computed by individual workers, whole departments, divisions or even plants. These indexes make it possible to compare performance on completely different kinds of jobs. Standard labor costing systems and incentive wage payment system are based on production standards.

In the case of studying the performance measures, it is said that stopwatch study helps in work measurement and thus through simultaneous performance rating might determine the normal time and determine elemental standards, observe and record actual time and determine elemental structure of operation for timing purpose. Whereas work sampling can be defined as the number of observations is proportional to the amount of time spent in the working or idle state and this method accomplishes the result of the stopwatch study. The main advantages of work sampling are:

- Many operations or activities which are impractical or costly to measure by time study can readily be measured by work sampling. An analyst is required for an operator or machine when continuous time studies are made.
- There is less chance of obtaining misleading results as the operators are not under close observation for long periods of time. When a worker is observed continuously for an entire day, it is unlikely that he will follow his usual routine exactly.

- It is not necessary to use trained time study analysts as observers for work sampling studies unless performance sampling is required. However, if a time standard or a performance index is to be established, then an experienced time study must be used.
- Work sampling measurements may be made with a pre-assigned degree of reliability. Thus the results are more meaningful to those not conversant with the methods used in collecting the information.

When the attempt is made to structure the problems of operations management, reality demands that we consider not only the complex interactions of the factors internal to the operations phase but, where appropriate, the interactions between the operations phase and other functions as well as the interactions with the environment systems. Thus, the planning of production rates, size of work force, use of overtime and planned inventories (commonly called aggregate planning and scheduling) demands a model that accounts for some of these interactions in setting production rates and employment levels for the upcoming period. The first and most obvious environmental factor is consumer demand which is in direct compensation with other enterprises. Part of the aggregate planning model must include a forecast as well as the feedback of information on our actual order flows. The production rates and employment level decisions are also dependant on interactions with the labor pool (since the decision might either call for hiring or layoff), on the raw material or equipment pools to facilitate the production rate decisions, and on the financing pool (since the decision may call for accumulation or drawing down of inventories). The co-ordination with other functional sub-systems is parallel; that is, marketing in the forecast problem, purchasing in the equipment and raw material problem and finance in the inventory, payroll, and purchasing problems.

Similarly while talking of a critical view known as sub-optimization, it can be done by taking a short-range view of maximizing profits or an organizational narrow gage view. It might be according to the rise and fall of the sales curve. With a broader horizon he would look for trends and seasonal variations and develop a production program to meet requirements over the longer term. The short-range view would be a sub-optimization, since it focuses only on the payroll costs but ignores the long-term effect and costs of production fluctuations and inventories.

Organizational sub-optimization is common where the production function and distribution function are operated separately as two separate businesses. The factory then will try to minimize its costs independently as well as the sales and distribution function. Thus sales and distribution will be faced mainly with inventory management, shipping and customer service problems and will try to minimize the associated costs. On the other hand the factory will be faced with minimizing production costs. Each sub-organization, optimizing separately probably will result in a combined cost somewhat larger than if the attempt were to made to optimize the combined system as a whole. The reasons are obvious and in minimizing the cost of inventories, the sales function will transmit directly to the factory most of the effects of sales fluctuations instead of absorbing these fluctuations through the buffer inventories; sub-optimization is the result. By co-ordination it is possible to have a balance between inventory costs and production fluctuation costs.

Quantity control over quantities produced is not exercised by simply setting production rates. There is a complex interaction between actual demand and its forecasted pattern, production rates and the size of the work force. The amount to produce in the upcoming planning period depends on the use of the most economical combination of equivalent capacities (such as existing inventories, regular production, overtime production, and additional production due to increased work force size) in relation to some reasonable time horizon for demand. If the planning time horizons are considered the seasonal demand peak, then the comparative costs of hiring workers and using overtime must be balanced against the costs of back-ordering and lost sales. Production rate and hiring decisions depend on the combination of capacities that minimizes these costs. The effective implementation of basic aggregate plans largely depends on how men and machines are actually utilized; that is how these resources are scheduled and controlled. In continuous production systems, changes in basic production rates and employment levels called for by the aggregate plan require a rebalancing of facilities and assembly lines to adjust to the new employment level and match the new output rates. Finally in terms of quantity control, the designs of both maintenance and quality control procedures are important. Both sets of procedures have an impact on the control of output levels since both are concerned with maintaining the reliability of the physical system. If equipment is not maintained in good working order, there will be interference with attaining the planned production quotas. Idle labor cost for an entire production line is caused due to machine break-down. Preventive maintenance programs and quality control procedures are very important to make it highly effective and put everything in line.

Aggregate plans and programs look towards preparing decisions for the upcoming period in the planning horizon, where detailed scheduling can proceed at the lower level within the constraints of the broad plan. It is important to develop some logical overall unit of measuring sales and output, for example representing an equal quantity regardless of the package style as in the beer industry or perhaps equivalent machine hours in some mechanical industries. In this case forecasting should be done for at least a year to find out the net output through the aggregate plans. An important plan is to isolate and measure the relevant costs and reconstruct these costs in the form of a model that will permit near optimal decisions for the sequence of planning periods in the planning horizon. For the present period implementation detailed plans and schedules must be prepared for the use of existing workforce and equipment. Based on forecasts of demand for the future periods setting of production rates and plans for use of overtime and inventories are prepared. Tentative plans look at size of workforce, production rates, subcontracting and overtime inventories. Intermediate range plans for products and capacity look at changes in product mix and projected capacity needs for equipment and manpower. Long-range plans for products, markets, and capacities helps in studies of markets and their locations as well as studies of the size and location of facilities. Considering the cost factors, change in size of the work force affect the total costs of labor turnover. When new workers are hired, costs arise from selection, training and lower production effectiveness. Large changes in the size of the work force may mean adding or eliminating an entire shift; the incremental costs involved are shift premium as well as incremental supervision costs and other overhead. If fluctuations are absorbed through changes in the production rate, overtime premium costs for increases and probably idle labor costs for decreases also will be absorbed.

The work force size together with the decision on production rate during the period then determines the required amount of overtime, inventory levels or back-ordering, whether or not a shift must be added or deleted, and other possible changes in operating procedure. The comparative costs which result from alternate decisions on work force size and production rate are also of great effectiveness in judging the effectiveness of the decisions made and the decision process used.

Another part of the aggregate plan arises when the capacity limits have been set, creating a set of capacity constraints which must be observed in the detailed schedule that is generated. Thus the allocation of the limited capacity to product types and sizes becomes an important economic problem. The product mix problem may be most complex in chemical industries such as oil refining where there are also interdependencies in the quantities of different products which can be produced. If more of one product, such as aviation gasoline is to be produced, then less of some other product must be produced by the very nature of the refining process. The profitability of various products may be different, and there are limits to the markets for each. The result is a complex programming problem to determine the best product mix. The interdependencies always exist in oil refining, for example, because the basic raw material, crude oil, can be processed into many different products and an increase or decrease in one always means a change in the quantities of some other products. In the mechanical industries the interdependencies between products are more likely to stem only from the capacity limits imposed by the aggregate planning decisions and, in some, instances by the capacities of time shared facilities which are used to produce a variety of types and sizes.

In constructing a schedule for an assembled product, we must work backward from the required completion dates of the end product, using the general concept of the schedule diagram. The schedule diagram takes the basic structure of assembly, subassemblies, parts fabrication, material procurement and relates them to a time scale. Beginning with the receipt of the customers orders, the schedule diagram shows the time schedules that must be met at the various stages of planning and scheduling, material procurement, parts fabrication, subassembly and assembly in order that the final product be shipped by the target date. For a complex product such as an airplane, a missile, or a complicated electronic component, such charts are necessary. For a complex engineered product, time also would have to be allowed for the product engineering design to be completed. By determining the required time for final assembly, we determine the due dates for the subassemblies. The time to produce subassemblies in turn establishes due dates for manufactured and purchased parts. In each instance these estimates of time requirements must allow for process time, move time and time between operations. These setback times determine when production must start and when purchase order for needed raw material and purchased parts must be placed to meet the scheduled completion dates. The actual schedule of parts subassemblies and final product is the due date for each stage of manufacture and assembly. Gantt charts and their modern counterparts help provide information about the production schedule. They measure progress against the schedule, the load on departments of individual machines, and the availability of equipment or manpower. The plans and progress are plotted in relation to time. A Gantt project planning chart may be used to map out a detailed plan to accomplish target objectives. In a Gantt chart manufacturing an assembled product so that the availability of parts for assembly dovetails with the fabrication and the assembly time required, as shown by a schedule diagram. As subsequent subassemblies are completed, they will be taken to the final assembly area. The schedule could undoubtedly be compressed further by applying the same overlapping schedule to the subassemblies in relation to the parts fabrication. The overall scheduling of this project depends in part on the availability of men, machines and materials.

Maintenance can be composed of various types. Utilizing preventive maintenance where practical so that critical parts are replaced before they fail. It is often possible to do this on second and third shifts and thereby not interfere with normal production schedules. Whether preventive maintenance is worthwhile or not depends on the distributions of breakdowns and the relation of preventive maintenance time to repair time. Providing for slack in the system at critical stages makes parallel paths more available. This makes excess capacity so some machines can be down without affecting the delay costs to any degree. The thing that makes maintenance expensive are the down-time costs. An optimal balance of costs requires a sizable percentage of idle time for the maintenance crew. The machine maintenance time is idle because the crew must be ready to answer service calls. However, the idle time can be used to some extent with fill in work that is not particularly pressing.

In measures such as quality control the detailed specifications of quality to be produced are set by the product designer when he determines materials to be used and their specifications, dimensions, tolerances, product capacity and service requirements. There is an interaction between what can be specified, what can be produced, and the cost of production. Thus there is a complex process of design for quality, production, design of the product and design of the production system itself each often affecting the other to some degree. The three sub-phases of quality control are centered around the inspection and control of the quality of incoming raw materials, the product inspection and control of processes and the inspection and testing for product performance. Quality control must extend into distribution, installation and use phases. Quality control is designed by policy, designed by engineers or produced, but total performance of the product in his hands. A perfectly conceived and produced item may be damaged in distribution to be improperly installed. Quality control is done through assessments and corrections in the statistical control chart or through acceptance sampling.

In the outline on production costs the basic costs are determined by the decisions made in the production design of products and the design of the production system to produce the products; that is, the selection of processes, the organization and design of jobs and work methods, and the location and layout of the system. In the operating phase certain decisions are made which determine how close we can approach the minimum or ideal costs. The overall production program is an attempt to achieve the ideals of original design through the determination of how we utilize our plant and equipment, our manpower and inventories and our program of maintenance. Cost control through a set of budgets and reports, attempts to set up current cost standards and holds the supervisor responsible for cost performance in order that he makes these decisions in the interest of the organization. Cost improvement results from continuous reexamination of layouts, methods, tools, materials, designs, etc, to effect improvements in these areas and from a revision of cost standards on which cost control is based. Many organizations have carefully thought out programs for cost improvement, either through the efforts of a professional methods engineering group or by tapping the latent source of ideas from supervisors and workmen.

Cost data from past performance are compared with figures for last week, last month, last year etc. The difficulty with these measures is that no indication can be given regarding what cost performance should have been. Last years data may be a poor standard or may represent excellent performance. In the case of performance in comparable situations sometimes two supervisors have nearly comparable jobs so that their performance can be compared. Particularly in multi-plant situations, comparisons among the plant as a whole, as well as among individual departments can be made. Since conditions never are completely comparable, there are dangers in assigning the reasons for the differences in cost performance to the capability of the supervision involved. Standard costs are determined from the analysis of the conditions and are meant to indicate what the costs should be, given standard conditions. For example, a standard material cost for a part stamped from steel sheet can be determined by a layout of the part from the size of the sheet of raw stock used. Poor utilization of the raw material would result in a higher than standard material cost. Defective raw materials would represent a nonstandard condition. Standard costs reflect what costs should be under certain assumed conditions. The difficulty is that the standard cost usually cannot reflect all the possible conditions that could exist, such as variations in load and the pressure to get out a high-priority job. Standard costs can approximate what costs should have been, allowing explanation of variances from standard conditions. Even when an organization has a formal cost control system based on standard costs, past performances and comparable situations are bound to be referred to as additional measures. Standard overhead costs include such a variety of expenses that it is difficult to make a general statement about their behavior. Obviously, some costs classified as overhead, such as depreciation and taxes, are not controllable by the production supervisors(although they are controllable to some extent by someone in the organization). On the other hand, many overhead expenses can be influenced by supervisors. We are interested in the behavior of these costs in relation to volume, so that cost standards appropriate for different levels of operation can be developed. Physical measures of volume are more satisfactory such as units, barrels or tons produced by specialized high volume departments or plants. Direct labor hours represent a good measure of volume for job shops or other activities where the products or services produced are not homogeneous. Direct labor dollars are less satisfactory as a measure since different periods may reflect an inflation of wage rates and sales level. The value of products shipped in dollars is even less satisfactory as a measure of volume because of inflationary effects as well as lags between sales and production or inventory changes.

 Cost improvement programs have been common in business and industry for many years. They have run the gamut of suggestion systems; formal training courses pitched to supervisors, other operating personnel, and sometimes even workers; departments of professional methods engineers and outright management directives making across-the-board reductions in line and staff personnel in order to lower expenditures. Perhaps the major difference between managerial hatchet work and a well thought out cost improvement program is that, in the indiscriminate chopping of expenditures, the assuming is made that cost and expenditure are synonymous terms, where cost improvement programs consider the balance of cost alternatives. Mere expenditure reduction may well result in less effective operation and net increase in unit costs. Formal improvement programs are designed to create creative thinking about work, layout, tools, materials flow that gives a net gain to the organization. Improving existing operations essentially involves the reapplication of many of the methods of analysis described earlier. This may be regarded as a continuous process of design and redesign of the production system to incorporate the latest techniques and technology.

There is a range of application for linear programming. At first production facilities are allocated when alternate routings are available. Given the unit machining time for the alternate machine routes, total hours available on the different machine classes, requirements for the number of each product, and unit revenue for each product, linear programming can give a solution which would maximize some profit function, minimize incremental cost or meet some other management objective. Allocation of limited funds to various items of inventory is to minimize losses from less than optimal inventory levels. Linear programming helps cure many blending problems. Ex-a paint manufacturer may need to prepare paint vehicles that are a blend of several constituents. The constituents such as oil and thinner are available in limited quantity and in commercial blends of fixed proportions. Costs per gallon of the various possible raw materials are known. The problem is to determine the amount of each raw material such that the required amounts for the new blends are obtained at minimum costs. Another problem where linear programming is used is procurement problem where a manufacturer wants to know which parts to make and which to buy to maximize profits within plant capacity restrictions or within basic policies to subcontract a given minimum amount. Where subcontracting with particular suppliers is limited by policy or supplier's capacity, competing bids may be programmed so that profit is maximized within the policy or capacity restrictions. Another area where linear programming is used is scheduling of production to meet sales forecast using inventory fluctuations and overtime work to absorb random and seasonal variations in load. The other programming methods used due to the limitations of linear programming are quadratic programming: which is an algebraic technique which makes it possible to approximate more closely the actual cost curves. Dynamic programming makes it possible to solve multistage programming problems where the decisions generated by stage 1 becomes a condition for stage 2. Ex-for scheduling production the amount a business plans to produce this month is dependant partially on how much they produced last month because of the possible accumulation or reduction of backlogs. This chapter is a brief determination of the concept of production economics and how people should think about the major basic concept.

Chapter 6

A More Advanced Form of Process Management and Industrial Management

(By Baisham Chatterjee)

Process determination is a key concept in industrial management. Their two major aspects are technological and sequential. In a more advanced outlook technology is the combination of labor, machines, processes, energy, and other inputs directly involved in the transformation of materials into products-a technology of transformation. Technology considerations occur at two levels-general technological feasibility considerations and the specific choice of equipment. Sequential considerations are those that aim at determining the most efficient relationships between processing steps. When these relationships are determined, the resulting sequence represents the flow of materials, in-process inventory and completed products. Decisions relating to the specific choice of equipment, its optimal sequential relationships, and the determination of the required quantity and type of machines or processes should be viewed as different facets of a complex investment problem. People deal with this highly interrelated problems as if they were separable only because it is easier to understand the individual problems and decisions separately before perceiving all of them as part of a more encompassing decision. Technological considerations include the development of new technologies, the refinement or improvement of existing technologies, and the acceptability of an existing technology. Obviously the need to develop a new technology presents significant and sometimes insurmountable problem. However, some products come into being only when new technologies are developed to make the manufacture of products possible or economically feasible. The costs of such new technological developments in time and dollars are similar to the cost commitments required for new product design and development.

Such developments results from many factors: new scientific discoveries, new technological advances in related areas, or the synthesis of previously separate discoveries or advances into a new technology.

Firms using existing technology should maintain a continuing interest in improving it as long as changes are economically desirable and the investment can be justified. The three most frequent motives for seeking improvements in existing technologies are to increase the output rate, reduce unit costs and improve the yield. Often when improvements are discovered, developed or adopted their use may be concealed from the firm's competitors. Trade secrets, the term applied to such practices, may represent a firm's greatest economic advantage over its competitors. The employment of existing technologies has a number of interesting facets. The use of widely known technology does not give a firm any technological advantage as such. But it tells thus that machines, labor skills and standard costs are more readily available and thus can be more accurately estimated.

In the case of technological evaluation-general technological considerations aim at determining the technological feasibility of equipment or processes, viewed from several perspectives. Is this particular machine or process capable of producing the results called for in the product design or service design specifications? And if the machine or process under consideration meets the requirement, what volume of output can be anticipated, assuming that specific operating conditions such as labor and material quality, maintenance, and operating hours are met? Machines and processes are employed for both economic and technical reasons. Conversion of inputs into outputs by using machines is often more economical than the employment of labor only. In some situations machine productions may be the only means of producing the desired output. The importance to and the impact of each labor-machine alternative on the entire production system must be weighed. Machines designed to produce a specific transformation requirement are referred to as special-purpose machines and are not easily converted to perform other jobs. For example, an engine block boring mill used to bore the cylinders of gasoline and diesel engine, is designed to perform this job with high efficiency and precision. Similarly general-purpose machines are designed to accommodate a wide range of transformation demands. Paint-sprayers, commonly available at equipment and department stores, are general-purpose machines because they can cover a wide variety of products with various types of coatings.

To measure as a system of production focus and to understand the production equipment selection criteria, there are few points to cover. Investment is a major decision criteria and is lower as a result of standard and simpler designs in a general purpose equipment and has high initial cost due to not being a mass produced product in case of a special purpose equipment. Similarly maintainability is better focused when parts are generally cheaper and skill requirements less; and thus this may require fewer repairs; and may be highly reliable because of long life and greater number in use in case of a general purpose equipment. In case of maintainability for a special purpose equipment it requires higher skills and greater reserve resources to minimize breakdown time; preventive and scheduled maintenance is generally required to increase efficiency. A general purpose equipment requires higher labor skills to run equipment and a special purpose equipment require high skills to set up equipment. Labor unit cost in case of a general purpose equipment requires higher non-mechanized nature of production cycle under control of operator. The special purpose equipment looks at the loading and unloading processes. General purpose equipment has a quality consistency which is generally lower because of impact of operator and a special purpose equipment has its quality consistency potentially high; which may be good or bad depending on setup and process monitoring. In case of a general purpose equipment the tooling requirements consists of jigs and fixtures required to obtain higher output and quality and in case of special purpose equipment tooling is generally part of equipment. To look towards the flexibility area general purpose equipment is basically more adaptable to a wider range of product and special purpose equipment is restricted because of location, linkage with other equipment, or built-in limitations.

Few ways of evaluating equipment and processes include: 1) labor and skill requirements 2) output or capacity needs 3) flexibility 4) compatibility with existing investment 5) financial considerations 6) maintainability.

Again there are few ways of making process technology changes. Their consideration is one approach to overall cost reduction. They include 1) environmental regulatory changes requiring a change in the technology used.2)changes in the product design, 3)changes in the volume of output required 4) economic obsolescence or equipment and process deterioration and 5)cost reduction.

The first type of technological change most often occurs in response to legislation or regulations promulgated by quasi-legislative governmental body like Environmental Protection Agency(EPA). Standards limiting pollutants, regulating working conditions, and promoting consumer protection may require a firm to change its production technology. These restrictions may apply to exhaust and smokestack emissions, the types and quantities of pollutants allowed in effluent pumped into waterways, the storage and handling of raw materials; and equipment, process and workplace design. The second type of change, a change in product design, comes about for several reasons. Competition may cause a firm to change its product design to avoid losing its share of the market. Product design changes may occur to prolong the growth stage of the product life cycle or to correct previous design decisions now judged as being unsatisfactory. Product improvement may also initiate different technology requirements. The third situation, changes to meet output requirements, may require more or less equipment but not different technology. Increased output requirements can also be achieved by increasing the speed or operating time of equipment. At this point of time for technology changes it is difficult to evaluate future needs for increased or decreased capacity, and decisions about anticipated increases have a critical effect on investment, particularly when additional capacity cannot be achieved fast enough to meet market demand. The fourth situation requiring technological change, economic obsolescence, and equipment deterioration results from equipments and processes which become economically inefficient compared to available replacements or which cannot be maintained because of unavailability of spare parts or skilled maintenance personnel. The last situation involving technological change involves cost reduction. Often lower production costs can be achieved by adopting lower cost inputs and using more technologically advanced equipment and process designs. Mechanized or automated equipment & processes and newer equipment for transferring and handling materials may reduce costs by increasing plant capacity; reducing rejects and rework; and decreasing operating labor skills, labor requirements and in process inventory. Cost reduction through the adoption of newer technology is not a simple solution for lowering production costs. New or more efficient technologies are associated with higher fixed investment cost with a n increase in the break-even point.

Evaluating processes and investment would include: technological feasibility, financial considerations, training for maintenance personnel, compatibility with existing facilities and size and weight limits imposed by plant and building. Except for situations where there is only one viable process or equipment alternatives, or where the investment is required to meet safety or legal requirements, the assessment of the firms financial risks receives top priority. Firms having very limited means to acquire new resources, have to choose among alternatives that require minimal additional investment.

Production management cost control, summarizes the discussion of costs that have effect on an organization and their important points are like: 1)costs that tend to increase in inverse proportion to the amount of effort put into cost control. 2) the amount of effort put into cost control tends to increase when business is bad and decrease when business is good. 3) when business is good companies tend to proliferate their activities and thus disproportionately increase their costs. 4) expenses rise to meet the amount of money available 5) expenses too often find shelter in the small print of budgets. Economic life is another factor that calculates the economic life of an asset that reflects the effects of obsolescence and there will be an alternative machine or process. A number of their approaches are: 1) use a common time denominator: four cycles of a machine having an economic life of 5 years and 5 cycles of a machine having an economic life of 4 years in order to calculate the PVA as a common way of calculation. 2)compare the alternatives over the shorter of the two economic lives and subtract the estimated resale value of the machines with the longer economic lives and the salvage value for those with the shortest lives. 3) assume that all the alternatives have the same economic life and adjust the figures of the longer-lived alternatives for their resale value at the end of the period. 4) use average cost per year for each alternative, in this the total present value of each investment over its economic life is computed and then divided by its expected economic life.

Unlike as I talked of in the last chapter, in this chapter I would include the modern advantages of Gantt charts and PERT and CPM. To continue the advantages of Gantt charts are as: 1)they are generally inexpensive to set up and require comparatively little training use. 2) they clearly show the schedule decided on for each job. 3) schedule changes in the plan can be made readily and at minimal cost. 4) the act of updating charts often gives the impetus necessary to exert control. 5) commercial chart boards are readily available for scheduling and control purposes.

The advantages of PERT and CPM are: 1) they allow project planning to any desired level of detail. 2) at the desired level of detail, the plan clearly indicates the intended order of accomplishment, the degree of inter-job dependency, and scheduling flexibility. 3) the chance of overlooking important jobs essential to successful project completion is drastically reduced. 4) job responsibility and the need for coordination are clarified. 5)a pictorial plan is provided, and a broader understanding of responsibilities by the participants is achieved. 6) management by exception is encouraged because only problem areas are highlighted. 7) cost-benefit analysis is available for decision-making about the merits of expediting specific jobs or an entire project.

If everything is to be used in the right manner then something that has to be reframed is known as capacity planning. Assuming that the product or service specifications are achieved, the capacity of a piece of equipment or process is measured in terms of its ability to produce a specified level of output within a given time frame, such as units per hour or tons per day. A common practice in capacity planning is to consider both present and future capacity requirements and provide space for present and future equipment and processing needs, but to install equipment that is sufficient only for current production needs. It is to achieve maximum plant capacity for future machines and processes. It depends on the maximum benefits earned and the success of the product which can be used for storage or other temporary uses. This eliminates the costly and disruptive requirements for future re-layout of facilities when additional capacity is required. It depends on the investment funds available and the cost of carrying this added investment as an overhead expense weighed against the future cost of adding the capacity, including a re-layout of the facilities. Capacity as it is outlined in the production system is of three perspectives: design or theoretical capacity, effective capacity, and actual or operating capacity. Design capacity represents the maximum output that can be achieved within a specific time period under ideal conditions. It may and commonly does include a recognition of the need for routine maintenance but does not include a recognition for delays caused by factors such as scheduling conflicts, defective product, low-quality materials, or changes in the product mix. Design capacity values are generally stated by the manufacturer of the equipment. Effective capacity represents the maximum output per unit time given a particular product mix, labor skills, supervision, product quality level, material quality, available maintenance and time between set-ups.

Product design affects capacity by determining the total work content or processing requirements for producing a part or product. Changes in design or a greater variety of products will generally affect capacity adversely by requiring more frequent changes in set ups, increasing rework, or requiring that equipment and processes be operated at lower speeds. The opportunities to increase effective capacity are greater when product design is simplified, changes are infrequent and production runs are long. The layout of facilities is an important determinant of effective capacity because of its effects on the flow of materials, in-process production and the effectiveness of labor. The presence or absence of adequate storage space for in-process production, the quality of raw materials, the availability of supplies, the provision of adequate and strategically located aisles for moving materials and products in and out of production areas and the need for adequate heat, light, and ventilation in processing areas also effect capacity.

The advantages of process layout are: 1)processing flexibility may be greater for efficiently producing a variety of products that require standard processes. Process layouts are less vulnerable to breakdowns or absenteeism than other types of layout since work can be shifted to other operating machines, and substitutes for absent employees are more readily available because employees have multiple skills. 2)lower capital costs may be realized from the use of general-purpose machines, which are less likely to become obsolete than special-purpose machines. 3)lower installation and maintenance costs may be realized if special requirements can be achieved such as isolating noisy machines and meeting special safety conditions. Through effective scheduling better use of maintenance skills and time can be achieved, resulting in lower maintenance costs, because excess capacity is often available. Another layout option relates to recent technological development of flexible manufacturing systems (FMS) where the direction in the manufacturing cells are done by computer controlled machines. Remotely guided carts deliver inputs to where they are needed, and robots unload the carts to waiting machines for processing.

Planning, pre-production i.e installation of operator methods and production i.e maintenance of operator methods are the important elements before starting production. Explicit consideration is given to the impact of other planning functions on the operator method design decision. The preproduction stage represents the turnover of methods developed in the first planning stage to the production department at the same time that equipment and processes are being installed and the production control procedures have been developed. In the meantime several resource commitments are made like-operator training; operator assignment; and a preproduction tryout of facilities materials and methods. The third stage i.e the production stage is where the refinements, and the refinements in methods design from the time of their introduction to the time when methods are significantly improved or replaced. The circular flow of the process including method specification, analysis for improvement, evaluation of alternatives, and methods revision should be seen as an ongoing organizational activity whose goal is to continually seek improvements in labor and machine productivity through policies that aim to prevent the maintenance of the status quo.

The design of products on the basis of different dimensions is the basis of developing and controlling operator methods. This further leads to design of processes on basis of operation sequence, location points, dimensions and tolerances. This is further related to design of operator method which is composed of flow, workspace, economic evaluation etc. Moreover design of plant layout is composed of location of stock supply, location of services like electricity and gas and man machine relationship. The merging of all these components relates to transfer of information and responsibility to production organization that occurs at the same time as these actions.

Two approaches that have been frequently successful in increasing output, improving quality, decreasing unit costs, improving employee satisfaction and reducing employee turnover are job enlargement and job enrichment. The Hawthorne effect or the Hawthorne experiment is an example of that. A meaningful job enrichment method helps in: increasing the accountability of individuals for their work that would further enhance the job scope and thus help concentrate on the main idea and remove all unnecessary controls. It is very important to carry out responsibilities with sufficient freedom and thus enhance through a competitive and expert mode the flow of information that workers receive. It is important to perform difficult tasks at high levels of expertise and bringing the other ideas together to handle them with specialized tasks.

Even as a key part of organization development: we look at job design as a description of individual tasks that must be done that decides the manner in which those tasks are to be performed and how specific jobs can be assigned to individual workers. Job content is an example which consists of specialization of skills that minimizes skill requirement and the combination of both reduces the learning time. Worker satisfaction and distribution of work are the integral component of job content. Situations where humans have an edge over machines are: the ability to respond to situations and storing and retrieving information to understand the responses very appropriately. It is important to understand common denominators in work situations and the necessity to respond to changing stimuli and the ability to understand the differences in the quality of inputs and to understand the recurring problems.

Similarly the advantages attributable to machines are: sensing stimuli like X-rays, radar wavelength and ultrasonic vibrations that are outside the normal human range of sensitivity. It is important to apply deductive reasoning, monitoring for pre-specified events that relates to storing and retrieving coded data in sufficient quantities. It is important to understand the input signals, perform repetitive outputs reliably, count and measure physical activities and perform several programmed activities simultaneously.

The optimal design of tools and equipment controls is essential to achieving labor and machine efficiency in man-machine production systems. The minimal criteria for designing both tools and equipment controls are that the tools, devices and controls are effective in performing the intended function and are compatible to anthropometric and biomechanical performance characteristics of the people who will use them. These two design criteria are always compatible because tools, devices and controls can be best used by people and fulfill their intended function. The design of equipment controls like hand wheels, levers and push buttons are manually moved by the operator to produce the necessary response from the machine or process of which they are parts. The desired control actions or responses can be verified by using lights, dials, meters and auditory displays. Rationales for not insisting on improved job designs and not providing a better work environment include such factors that don't lead to output maximization and cost minimization, because people start thinking of it too much when the cost is prohibitive. It is not always successful because management expects new machines, processes and activities to be replaced before they pay for themselves. Its difficult to think of processing requirements and there is no alternative technology to reach towards the goal. The unit production cost of labor and capital are weighed in favor of maximizing machine or process efficiency. Restrictive clothing similarly bring inefficient methods or prohibits methods from the standpoint of production.

Similarly taking the case of inventories, the existence of inventories permits retailers, at least for a short time, to be independent of the firm's production capacity. Product design, process selection and capacity planning relate directly to inventories. Product design specifications stipulate the types and the quality of the materials and parts that make up the product. Inventories to meet independent or dependent demand situations obviously must meet the requirements stipulated in the product specifications. Decisions about process selection and capacity planning also relate directly to inventory planning and control. The choice of equipment may require that the material inputs be of a particular size, shape, weight or texture for processing to be efficient. Machines such as lathes or milling machines require that the stock of raw materials be cut to meet the size limitations of the machines or be purchased so as to meet these limitations. The capacity of machines and processes is influenced by the quality of inputs and the time required to perform the necessary processing steps. Differences in the required processing time may be due to the quality and consistency of the raw material inventories. When inventories are inadequate to meet processing requirements, the effective capacity of the processing system is correspondingly reduced.

Labor skills affect inventory planning by directly influencing the level of defective product produced. Inadequate labor skills or training resulting in high reject levels will reduce processing capacity and require higher levels of materials purchases and higher inventories which will be translated into higher production costs. Managerial competence which is a labor skill, translates into minimal inventory costs through properly planned, designed, controlled and managed processes. Finally, the acquisition, maintenance and control of inventories is not generally assigned to operations and operations managers. The responsibility for actually ordering raw materials, parts, supplies and products is most often assigned to the purchasing department. The authorization for the purchase of such items may come from production control, production planning, or the materials management function. The transfer of items into inventory may be the responsibility of the purchasing department, which functions as a receiving department, or a separate group associated with production control or materials management. Withdrawals from inventory very frequently are authorized by departments or groups such as inventory control or materials management. Operations managers do not make decisions concerning inventory levels; they have little direct say as to the quantities ordered, the choice of suppliers, or the mode of transportation and they are not involved in price negotiations. Interruptions in the supply of raw materials or in-process product may require rescheduling or cancelling orders if they cannot be completed on time, storing-in-process product that cannot be completed, correcting or changing work schedules, and reprocessing or reworking unsatisfactory product as a result of using deteriorated inventories.

Inventory turnover is another criteria that determines production function which refers to the number of times an item in inventory has been replaced during a given period, or stated somewhat differently the number of times during a given period that the average investment in inventory is sold. The common assumption that high inventory turnover rates imply high profits is not necessarily true. If inadequate stock is carried so that new stock must be ordered more frequently, the result will be a higher turnover rate. This may also lead to higher ordering costs, higher transportation costs and lower customer service levels. On the other hand, low inventory turnover usually indicates the presence of excessive levels of inventories relative to demand, which implies a higher than necessary investment of working capital. After taking this as a point another important factor i.e lead time can be defined as the interval between placing an order for products, parts, or materials and receiving them. Then for internally produced parts or products, lead time may be defined as the total time required to obtain the required raw materials and purchased components; perform the required processing, fabrication and assembly steps; and package and ship the goods to other locations within the firm or to customers. Similarly stock-out costs are incurred when demand exceeds inventory levels. The costs associated with running out of inventory includes loss of customer goodwill, process shutdowns, and any action taken to avoid or minimize the severity of stock-outs. Where customer goodwill exists, an adequate customer service level also exists. Shutdowns occur when needed inputs for a production process do not arrive on time. Shutdowns result in additional start up or set up costs. Actions taken to avoid or minimize the effect of stock-outs include expediting production and transportation and choosing a higher priced but available source. The inventory costs can be divided into two parts: ordering costs and storage and carrying costs.

Ordering costs include the costs of writing purchase requisitions, purchase orders and associated accounting costs as well as cost of receiving and inspection. It is obvious that to minimize ordering costs, one has only to order large quantities very infrequently. However by pursuing low ordering costs, one may well incur high inventory holding costs. Unit ordering costs are a function of the order size, and they decrease as the quantity ordered increases. The determination of the best trade-off between ordering and holding costs is the basis for the classical inventory models. Storage and carrying costs are the costs associated with owning and maintaining inventories. Storage cost include heat, light, rent, building taxes, warehouse maintenance including janitorial services and plant protection. Carrying costs include inventory taxes, recordkeeping, inventory insurance, loss from obsolescence and theft and interest charges on the capital invested in inventory. Based on the space occupied by the specified inventory item, storage costs can be charged. Records of carrying and storage costs are generally based on average inventory, which includes any safety or buffer stock and is expressed as a percentage of the average inventory value.

By looking at the choice of inventory models, the costs of ordering and holding inventories includes criteria's that formulate the policies and strategies include changes in the perceived reliability of present vendors that assesses probabilities of inventory sources being unable to deliver on time because of labor stoppages or shortages, restricted capacity or financial problem. Moreover changing the firm's objectives, policies, and strategies in regard to the relative importance of customer service, builds the firm's image, costs and employment stability. If resources are getting scarce then it is very important that through due time, environment and further research and competition consumer preference changes. Due to technological changes in the industry and in closely related industries, national, regional and industrial expectations change. To bring development in inventory levels there should be a careful and descriptive study of the present financial health of the firm and look at the changes in the activities, services and products offered by competitors.

In case a firm reviews its inventory policy regarding a particular product. Suppose also that it is anticipating a working capital shortage and an increase in foreign competition and has some recent unresolved problems involving the quality and dependability of deliveries from a particular vendor. The prospect of increased foreign competition may take the form of price, quality, service, function, aesthetics or some combination of these factors. If it could be determined that price and service constituted the competitive edge for the foreign producer, the firm's response in regard to inventory policy might include seeking to obtain lower resource prices, decreasing the capital investment, shifting the responsibility and financial burden for holding for employing more effective controls. A shortage of working capital would be expected to push the firm in the direction of decreasing inventory levels and installing new inventory, production and cost controls and tightening existing ones. This may improve profit margin with a reduction in unit price.

The products a firm makes will determine the types of inventory it must have and will influence the inventory policy and the system of inventory control employed. The materials, supplies, purchased parts, labor and managerial skills, and equipment and facilities are all heavily influenced, if not specially determined by the product design decision. The types of equipment and facilities will define the types of maintenance, inventories of skills, spare parts, and equipment required while the utilization rate for the production processes employed will affect the quantity of resources needed to maintain a specified level of capacity. If the utilization rate for a particular process is high, the demand for maintenance skills necessary to keep it functioning properly will be higher than for a lower utilization rate, and there will be greater need for spare parts and maintenance supplies. The idea of requiring a different approach to planning, designing or controlling inventories for situations where demand for parts, components or subassemblies is derived from the demand of the end product also requires some explanation of what these special conditions are and what justifies a different approach. When the demand for a product or service is known with considerable certainty, as in the case where an agreement or contract between a producer or customer or user exists, the demand for the components, parts, supplies and materials that go into making, assembling or processing of the product should be known to the same degree of certainty. The product or service specifications. Blueprints, and material lists contain the requisite information for fabrication or assembly.

Materials requirement planning is an important sub-part of inventory management where materials requirement planning seeks to achieve three major goals: where the first starts with minimizing inventory investment, maximizing the efficiency of production system and lastly it is improving customer service. Minimizing the inventory investment deals with bringing the correct resources as required by the product or service specifications. Similarly it is a responsibility to look at the quantities necessary to meet production schedules-recognizing that there may be trade-offs such as that between order quantity and total unit costs. At a correct time it is important to meet production schedules and minimize inventory investment and holding cost. The second goal of MRP, to maximize the efficiency of the production system, is achieved by proper planning. Planning will first require determination of production schedules based on the availability of resources and capacity and then maintaining schedule priorities by keeping abreast of any changes in planned material order arrivals and production order status. Expeditious material resource procurement may be less disruptive than expediting production at a later time and then having to inform customers that their orders will be delayed. By keeping informed of the status of material procurement and production orders, the problems associated with scheduled changes can be more effectively handled. Actual and effective capacity of the production system will be increased by reducing scheduling conflicts and schedule gaps. Material requirements planning is most effective where: A relationship can be easily developed between a multistage production system to better understand how to reject allowances that are nonexistent or small and predict the quality level. Independent demand represents a very small portion of total demand and brings a minimal variation in procurement lead times. Forecasts of the finished product are good enough that feasible master schedules can be developed and followed from it. Similarly a large proportion of the activity is in assembly in case of MRP rather than fabrication. This technique and technology helps in large yearly output and a job shop multiproduct production system is employed. It is doubtful whether firms seeking an alternative to present poor management practices in planning for materials requirement and in inventory control can fully benefit from going to a computerized system. All computer based MRP systems require managerial discipline if they are to be employed successfully. Inventory records must be accurately maintained and feasible master schedules made out on time. Both inventory records and master schedule will probably require new formats and more accurate and timely data collection techniques to accommodate the requirements of a computer. Old ways of handling paper controls and the ability to adjust and interpret figures will in large part, be lost when going to MRP. The old job approach will be replaced by more of a line approach with all the problems of interdependency among functions impacting on planning and production efficiencies and on the quality of the reports generated. Success for a poorly managed firm going to MRP may represent more of an improvement over the unacceptable past than an actual achievement of an efficient and effective system of materials management. Kanban is an inventory approach performed by Japanese automobiles and this approach is applied to vendors as: Suppliers that encourage to locate near the firm to reduce the firm's transportation costs and lead time. Moreover in this case orders from suppliers to the firms are produced in small lots and shipments are made frequently. Buffer inventories are the responsibilities and obligation to suppliers and because suppliers are a firm's single source for a particular part or product, they enjoy a large volume of business. Suppliers with larger volumes of business can often reduce their own purchasing and inventory costs, which in turn reduces their breakeven volume and increases their profitability. Technical and financial assistance may be available to the firm's suppliers to enable them to develop into dependable sources of high quality, low cost parts or products. Parts and product quality is demanded and achieved by the firm because of the economic dependence of the suppliers and the lack of inventories to fall back on if mistakes are made.

Under the impetus of an economic recession we presently see an increased awareness of managers in the automobile and other similar industries of a need to take a broader and longer-run view of their inventory management responsibilities. They are finding that while in the short-run many of the inventory management parameters are fixed, they can be advantageously changed in the long run if conventional wisdom gives way to objective analysis. Product design encapsulates the firm's present concept of quality as it reflects and compromises among costs, manufacturing ability, market competition, employer training and the firm's ability to control its production processes. The process that culminates in the design of a product commits the firm to the acquisition of machines, processes, materials, and labor skills capable of meeting the product specifications noted in the product design. Manufacturing activity reflect and implement policy in decisions made for the procurement of raw materials, process development, training for quality and the control of quality. Marketing activity provides quality determining inputs into the product design process when competitors products are evaluated and when market needs are assessed.

To look at the inspection procedures in production, there are two types of attributes: inspection for attributes and inspection for variables. Inspection for attributes consists of identifying important product attributes or characteristics and developing a means of determining whether a particular attribute exists for a given part or product that is called for in the design specification. Examples of inspection for attributes are the separation of steel washers for bolts into two groups or lots-those with holes and those without-or the separation of a manufacturing run of light bulbs into those which light up when tested and those which do not. Inspection of variables requires making measurements of certain characteristics of a part or product. These measurements can generally be expressed in terms of a continuous scale. Whether one chooses attribute or variable sampling depends on the objective. Generally if design specifications call for large tolerances such as those commonly employed in manufacturing steel washers, one would probably use attribute sampling technique whether one was monitoring or ongoing process, checking the product after it has been made, or checking a vendor-supplier lot. There are many factors affecting inspection decisions: they are as on automatic process equipment at first items are produced to check the set-up, take periodic samples as required during the run and inspect the last unit processed. Inspect before costly or irreversible operations to avoid additional costs and multiplying costs.

The sequence of processing steps required and the applicable labor and material standards that will enable production control to schedule, plan, and control production quantities, timing and costs originate in the process and industrial engineering departments. The inventory of raw materials and parts required to fabricate or assemble the products needed to replenish inventory stock or to meet customer demand will have to be ordered by purchasing through requests initiated by production control or inventory control personnel. Sometimes the inventory control is assigned to production control. Although specified in the product design, the quality standards are implemented by the production department and monitored by quality control personnel as products and parts are being produced. The material, parts, and product allowances for wastage that consume valuable capacity originate in the process engineering, industrial engineering and cost control departments. It is important to initiate orders and provide authorization to produce the quantity and quality of goods required. To carry out this responsibility the production control department should analyze orders to determine resource requirements and match these requirements with available capacity. Production control will, having made such an analysis, inform the sales department what fabrication or assembly and delivery dates are feasible for customer's orders. Provide the production department with routing information specifying manufacturing sequences, machine and process setup requirements, applicable labor work standards, and machine or processing time. Similarly it is important to initiate production orders that authorize and direct production personnel to make the required parts or products. There are different sub-divisions of this analysis where in one it is important to assist the efficient utilization of material resources, people and facilities. To achieve this the requirements are: providing the requisite order scheduling information to the production department on raw material, tooling, labor and machine requirements by synthesizing information obtained from different manufacturing departments. In a production control system it is important to initiate purchase orders and maintain and control raw material inventories. Other processes are developing order schedules and develop its cost and time estimates and provide detailed information on fabricating and assembling products. The production control reports requires to initiate the paper controls to provide feedback information on the status of orders. Compare work accomplishments with scheduled requirements to identify orders falling behind schedule or underutilization of facilities. A leadership role can also be assumed to provide the most accurate customer information, assist in developing master schedules and initiate corrective action in cooperation with production personnel.

Production control's responsibility effectively and efficiently aid the organization's achievement and resources according to the allocation requirements. Although production control does not engage in the primary effort of forecasting, it is intimately involved with the plans and schedules predicted in doing such forecasts. Long-run aggregate planning is a requisite for the design, development, and maintenance of continuing organizational efforts, including production control. Long-run planning gives specific purpose and direction to the production control by defining its organizational role and the scope of its specific responsibilities. Within the aggregate plan of the anticipated organizational activity based on the sales forecast, a number of other interrelated plans and schedules will be developed. It creates operating plans and schedules, production control must analyze the resource requirements for each product and part order and match the requirements against the availability of materials, labor and processing capacities. If capacity or other resources are not available then required by the customers order delivery date these problems must be worked out by changing the priority of orders in the system, or with the concurrence of the customer scheduling the order earlier or later. Before a sales order constitutes production authorization, the sales, production and engineering must determine whether it can be made, when it can be made and what the cost of making it would be. For new products all the three departments should supply the answer. In the customers request for a bid the bid may require the successful bidder to design the product and manufacture it. The price the firm quotes to the customer will determine whether the firm will receive an order. The customer's bidding process may very well require that the successful bidder deliver the product on some specified date in accordance to the agreed schedule. The tentative scheduling of an order may cause other problems for the firm. If the sales department is successful in obtaining additional orders as well as those on which it bids, the production capacity of the firm might be exceeded. If it refuses an order to be fabricated during a allocated period and the first bid does not materialize, the firm would either have to reschedule the orders or find them with excess capacity. The relationship between sales, costs, capacity and the master schedule can be seen as a dynamic one requiring close cooperation, coordination and information exchange among the firm's production control, sales, engineering and its customers.

Another significant area that leads to production control is maintenance. Time lost because of maintenance may interfere with schedules for strategy implementation. Finally, maintenance requirements should be considered in choosing equipment for replacement or expanding capacity and therefore have a direct impact on the overhead costs charged to the products and services a firm produces. Maintenance of facilities, equipment and processes is performed by a firm's maintenance department. The authority of maintenance to be performed generally lies with the operations department. The choice of who will actually maintain equipment or processes is determined by policy. Very often special skills and knowledge required are not present within the company's maintenance and when equipment is under warranty outside maintenance personnel are often used. Maintenance responsibilities assigned may include building maintenance such as painting, repairing, and remodeling, external plant maintenance, such as care for grounds, parking lots, and fences and general maintenance functions such as window washing, electrical power distribution etc.

There are basically three interdependent approaches to maintaining equipment, processes and plant. The first is often referred to as breakdown maintenance and requires the maintenance department to respond to situations in which the equipment or processes is not functioning or has been shut down because it is judged that they are about to fail, are producing unacceptable output or are unsafe. The basic responsibilities of the maintenance department are to diagnose the problem, plan to correct it and perform the required maintenance. The second approach is preventive maintenance. The essence of this approach is to perform maintenance in anticipation to actual need. Rather than wait for a machine to fail, this approach uses statistical analysis of past equipment performance to predict when failure is imminent. Then preemptive action is taken to perform the necessary adjustments in repair. A third approach is predictive maintenance. As the name implies, this approach involves using sensing devices to determine the internal condition of equipment and processes. It is analogous to a person having a thorough physical examination. through the measurement of factors such as noise emission, vibration, temperature, changes in output, waste products, use of lubricants, pressures and changes in electrical resistance, an interference can be made regarding the internal condition of the equipment. The predictive maintenance can be advantageously used in conjunction with preventive maintenance to signal the need to advance the time for performing scheduled maintenance or to provide an objective rationale for delaying scheduled maintenance. The decision to emphasize preventive or breakdown maintenance over the other depends on many factors such as the overall cost of maintenance, safety; consequences of interruptions; importance of particular processes or equipments to the production system; the extent to which processes are decoupled; the cost of lost production; and the size, skills, and experience of maintenance department. Often maintenance is performed in more than one stage, as in cases where an entire unit or module is replaced.

When a failed unit or module of a larger and more complex process is replaced, the immediate requirement for maintenance has been met by returning the equipment or process to operating condition. In case of a maintenance policy or maintenance program when a firm is small, a breakdown approach to maintenance may make economic sense and are assessed in terms of firms increasing in size in due comparison to their maintenance departments. As in case of a breakdown maintenance policy which sometimes cannot be anticipated with a high degree of certainty, a larger than optimal maintenance work force is often retained. To increase maintenance efficiency through reducing idle time, product management is often introduced. Equipment downtime can often be reduced by replacing modules and having maintenance personnel repair the units removed as time permits.

The frequency of maintenance means just what the phrase states. Depending on the type of maintenance that will be performed, a frequency will be established on the basis of an equipment history indicating need, informed estimates, or the manufacturing recommendations. The time may be in days, weeks, months and years. The major and subcontract groups refer to the maintenance group that is assigned the major responsibility for maintaining the equipment and other specific groups that are to be involved. In case of the direct current for the contract group would likely be electrical department and the sub-contract group might be electrical and mechanical maintenance. The job plan for a particular unit refer to a general maintenance activity such as lubrication or to a specific repair, overhaul procedure, or plan formulated especially for the machine or process.

All too frequently operations or manufacturing is perceived to be less important to a firm's profitability, survival or growth than the functions of marketing, finance and engineering. If we assume a set of objectives for a firm and develop a set of compatible strategies for their attainment within the guidelines of the policy, the operations function must be recognized as essential to the success of any strategy. A goal of increasing the use value of a product, will require a cooperative effort of engineering design, production control and operations. A decision by top management not to finance more efficient and effective equipment processes, will often be overlooked be overlooked in the short run because if the alternatives and opportunities are not recognized, there will be no new standard to measure tomorrows performance. Design changes that simplify a design from a manufacturing standpoint may be desirable from a marketing standpoint may also be cost-effective.

Technology change may be brought about by introducing a single invention or by the synthesis of a number of inventions. It may occur in service as well as manufacturing. Office changes from typing to word processing or from manual to mechanical accounting systems to computer-based systems represent technological change. In manufacturing the use of numerically controlled processes and machines, the employment of robots for fabrication and inspection, equipment and product designs and introduction to new methods and new materials all represent technological change. Organizational structures are often hastily and radically reorganized with changes in strategy, changes in top management, or when adverse changes occur in the firm's financial condition. Under more competent management, changes in organizational structure, which are necessary to orchestrate technological change and innovation, should be of a more evolutionary process than a revolutionary one. It is in the operations areas that innovations and technological change may come most frequently and with greatest impact. Technological change, in contrast to organizational change, may, because of its less predictable nature and timing, require more rapid introduction and present management and supervision with the dual problem of when and how to introduce it. Strategies that require the implementation of technological change should be carefully planned to achieve an acceptance of the required changes from the supervision and management levels.

Confidential information includes information on new technology, changes in the need of technology, process and equipment employed, levels of rejects, costs, trade secrets, operating methods, productivity records, and the firm's interest in and pursuance of new products, methods and materials and the firm's general as well as specific organizational and technological problems. Confidential information has certain subcategories like: information that will likely damage the firm's competitive position if revealed. Information which would adversely affect the firm's public image and information that would weaken a firm's position when dealing with a union, customers, suppliers. Information security limits the dissemination of information on a need-to-know basis and prevents the theft of information by company employees or outsiders. Further the dispatch of this information is controlled by such factors like the mobility of workers and rapid development of industrial technology, and achieving accurate timely information through immense technological and financial gain by competitors from acquiring accurate and timely information, especially in high-tech industries. Communication security is concerned with safeguarding information transmitted orally, in writing, by electronic means, or by means of sample materials or products. Control of information may be obtained by limiting access to proprietary information, restricting the means of communication, restricting the means of duplicating information and strict accounting for written documents. Technological security aims at protecting information from individuals or groups who use devices as radio transmitters, telephone taps, telescopic microphones and other sophisticated ways of listening to conversation and other sound related communication. The value of secrets, technological limitations, availability of resources and human resourcefulness, initiative and ingenuity define the boundaries within which outsiders will seek to gain the proprietary information. The art or practice of intelligence must be viewed as a two-way street with each from seeking the information it needs while providing the competitors with as little as possible.

Organizations attempt to reduce risks or uncertainty through various means like gathering and evaluation of information. The basic knowledge behind the environment in which a firm operates includes information on competing and substitute products, consumer trends, sources of raw materials and parts, costs and competitive strategies. Information services like company catalogues, periodicals includes information on a company's hiring of workers and managers, particular skills, new products, volume of sales, manufacturing methods and distribution channels, changes in product volumes and capacity estimates etc. Sources of information other than published materials include new employees, intercompany contacts, products, company salesmen and vendors. Intercompany contacts are made primarily by a company's professional staff, salesperson and executives. Technocrats, designers and researchers attend professional meetings for social reasons and as part of their continuing professional education. For firms dependant on or subject to rapid technological change, professional staff personnel present the greatest potential for losing proprietary information and at the same time are probably most competent to judge the value of information coming into their possession.

For a firm producing a product or service whose competitive advantage lies in the trade secrets and proprietary information, the preservation of the confidentiality of that competitive edge should be a conscious effort. If a firm in a service industry sees that its competitive advantage lies with how it is organized, it leads the firm to see organizational charts, job descriptions and compensation plans not available to competitors. Advantages based on products used in performing services might justify disguising them by repackaging, removing labels, or buying in bulk or under a generic label. If the firm manufactures a product, care should be taken that evidence of the existence of trade secrets is not revealed by examination of the product. This might be achieved by disguising the evidence, covering it up with a finish, or providing false clues such as quoted serial number blocks. To reduce risks and lower costs, all organizations should attempt to reveal as little as possible in the way of proprietary information and learn ethically about the competition. There is a great amount of information and data available in the environment in which a firm operates, selecting formal intelligence team for collecting; analyzing and evaluating information on competitors employment skills and development interests, organization structure, products, methods, and expansion plans. It is important to provide information for product design, process and equipment acquisition and research and development decisions. Thus the work of intelligence requires both training and experience.

Chapter 7

Construction management
(by Baisham Chatterjee)

There can be various types of construction work, the major being building dams and cannel. The work was usually bid on unit prices-i.e prices were submitted on such items of work as common excavation per cubic yard, rock per cubic yard, concrete per cubic yard, and reinforcing steel and structural steel gates and gate guides per pound or per ton. Similarly a joint venture is a limited partnership between 2 or more contractors covering a single job. The purpose of the joint venture is to spread the risk (as the jobs became larger, as a contractor going alone could go broke on a single job). Another important part is to reduce the amount of financing required from each partner, to get the advantage of each partner's judgment in pricing the work. Dam builder first practiced the charting and scheduling of the sequence and timing of all major items of work. Equipments and plant were furnished to meet a preplanned schedule. Canal work requires careful planning and from 18 months to 36 months but if the canal was unlined very little equipment was required per dollar of contract volume. Highway work similarly is not as long term as most other heavy construction and is the least profitable of all. For grading, surfing and paving a little amount of equipment is required. The amount of equipment required doesn't vary with the size of the job and includes tractors with dozers, ruber-tired scraper units, trucks, shovels, draglines, cranes, discing and harrowing tools, sheepsfoot and rubber-tired rollers, black hoe for digging structures, steel forms for concrete pavement with pavers and spreading tools, vibrators, finishing machines. In bridge construction a few companies specialize in it to the exclusion of other work, but most bridges are built by highway or diversified contractors. Since many contracts carry rather simple bridges with shallow piers and little or no hazard along with highway work, the general contractor will elect to sub-contract his bridges, culverts and structure concrete to one or more subcontractors who specialize in this work, and thus avoid organizing for this portion of the contract. Industrial building construction is in itself a whole series of specialty fields. Some types of industrial construction are open to medium-sized contractors of focal or regional scope. Large warehouses, airline mechanical bases and even tire plants and automobile assembly plants often are awarded on competitive bids. Sometimes the architect-engineer is designated as construction manager and for a fee prepares plans and specification, contracts the work to one or a number of different other contractors, and acts as inspector as well as designer.

Contracts are secured by negotiating with the owner, the chairman or president or in some cases the chief engineer. The contractor in determining the approach to the owner must know what proposal to present. Frequently a meeting with the owner or top officer whom he has designated to receive proposals, analyze them, and recommend award will pay off. If he maintains a competent engineering department or has employed outside architects, which may issue a complete set of plans and specifications which will state firm price, in lump sum or in units. The proposal must be presented in time. There are many functions in engineering. When someone looks at the purchasing and equipment management function certain major orders and major job purchase commitments had to be made with the presidents approval and even to a degree with his handling. He could sometimes get a little extra discount on cement and or explosives or perhaps on reinforcing bars or structural steel by talking to top officers of the vendor company. The engineering manual states that, previously designated office engineer was promoted to assistant chief engineer. He received no other title for policy reasons and his duties were outlined in the manual. On projects of any size a cost engineer is usually provided. He has to advise the job personnel and headquarters on the current costs and projections on all phases of the project. Unless the company has key executives with sound background and broad knowledge of mine and mill construction and operation, chemical, metallurgical, refinery or manufacturing plants, as well as access to engineering organization for design in the field, the company may well hesitate to enter the competition. Building of such an organization from scratch is almost prohibitive. Opportunity lies to design and construct, and turnkey contracts. The success in private-owner sector is making high-level sales and they back them up with personable and competent key executives and an ample of inspectors.

By taking the influence of competition a shrewd analysis of the probable competition and its potentials in deciding whether to submit a proposal on a given project, and prior to bidding if the decision is affirmative. A straightforward project has good climate, supervised by reasonable engineers. In the case of over caution an excess of caution can cause the contractor to pass up a very good job. To pass out the dam in favor of more complicated but less attractive subway work had been most successful. In the influence of experience the decision having been made to submit a proposal on a given contract and adequate study ascertains fundamentals affecting cost, the final decision on bid price, target price or guaranteed max hinges on how someone is likely to approach the particular job. Bidding propaganda between competitors sometimes takes the form of elaborate planning and skillful execution. When proposals are called on for major projects away from the population centers or bids are scheduled to be opened away from the site of work, an engineer district or division headquarters, naval districts or state capitols, they gather at one of the more leading hotels to pick up any available gossip. Additionally bidders are sometimes provided with pre-bid information or data, such as materials information pamphlets, soils reports, geological data, test of drilling reports. On public works projects, literal, formal, and absolute strict adherence to bidding requirements is essential to avoid possible rejection or disqualification of the bid and loss of a potential contract. The most important type of contracts is the fixed price or lump-sum contracts. The contractor wants to perform the entire work specified in the contract as a price agreed to and fixed at the time the contract is entered into. Competitive bidding is required over here. Where competitive bidding is not required by law, it is also possible to arrive at a fixed price by negotiation between the parties of the contract without resort to competitive bidding. A fixed-price contract is normally contrasted with cost-plus contracts, in which the price is determined by actual costs as they are incurred plus whatever additional payment in the way of a fee for profit. A variant of the fixed-price contract is the unit price contract. Some contractors consider unit price contracts as a separate species different from lump-sum or fixed-priced contracts. An example, a highway construction contract typically contains some items for which a lump sum or fixed price for the entire item is required, but there are many items which are contracted for a unit price basis, such as roadway excavation per units of volume, aggregate base material by weight or volume, concrete for pavement for volume, fencing or pipe by units of length. Such a contract consists of approximate quantities and a bidder is required to quote the unit price and is told to extend the price for each such item. In case of supplementary schedules, cash budget or equipment projections. In this the cash budget represents the company's estimate of the cash required to run the jobs and meet the various overhead commitments. This forecast is best prepared on a monthly basis for the first year of the project and then perhaps on a quarterly basis beyond this point. The forecast should indicate the maximum amount of financial requirement necessary to complete the job, when it will occur, and how soon after the project is completed the loan will be retired completely. When the loan officer is reviewing the equipment projections, he must give careful consideration to the costs of the preventive equipment maintenance. Much of the complex machinery used in large construction projects requires expensive maintenance at regular intervals if it is to remain operational for the life of a contract and into the future. Two items of cost must be considered: the out of pocket costs of maintaining the piece of equipment and the cost of time lost when the machine is not operating due to maintenance programs. If a giant earth moving machine must be overhauled for a month, the last month's work may represent thousands of dollars in delays and schedule re-adjustments.. The projected profit on a job may disappear if an expensive piece of equipment is destroyed.

When a contractor has an opportunity to bid a contract of a size or nature he does not feel that he should undertake alone, the common practice today is to create a joint venture with another contractor or several contractors. It is a temporary partnership for performing a specific contract. Profits and losses are shared on the basis of percentage of interest. They are severally bound to complete the entire contract and to pay all obligations incurred in doing so. It is related to unit type joint venture where one contractor does one part of the work and the other contractor the other part. In the case of equipment maintenance in an organization, success or failure depends upon the skill of personnel. High-caliber supervision and well trained workforce are needed. Beyond this is the need for team commitment to service-a sense of urgency in accomplishing the work and pride in doing it well. To build this type of organization is the real challenge of management. Personnel requirements for equipment maintenance organizations will vary with the scope of the job. Work specialization will increase proportionately with size of project and equipment fleet. In smaller operations the owner, operator or a single mechanic may function all maintenance functions. Basic considerations in establishing an equipment maintenance organization are size of the operation, type of equipment and type of work. Usually the number of maintenance personnel and supervisors needed depends on these factors. In a small operation, the machine owner assembles a team of versatile employees who have overlapping capabilities and responsibilities. It is important to note whether the book-keeper is full time or part time. With the help of accountant or book keeper costs can be analyzed and activities geared to improve profit. Requirements for field maintenance equipment will vary greatly with size and location of the site, the type of heavy machinery used and the work schedule of the operation. On small jobs, a constructor may use a single truck for fuel, lubricants, tools, filters, water and all other supplies. The expense of on-site service facilities is warranted only when the project is of sufficient size or duration or is too remotely located to be serviced from a home base. Whenever on-site service facilities are planned, they must be located a safe distance from other structures—away from the job traffic to avoid dust and congestion, yet easily accessible. The fueling truck should be equipped with high capacity fuel pumps to reduce filling time which is advantageous if earth moving machines are equipped with fast fill systems. Similarly the lubrication truck in the time of maintenance should be equipped to provide all oils and greases and other expendable items, such as filter elements, required for routine maintenance of the equipment fleet. Lubricants required in large quantities such as engine and hydraulic and cooling water or antifreeze solutions, should be carried in built in tanks of suitable size.

Preventive maintenance is the term applied to all phases of field maintenance when they are properly planned, properly performed and properly recorded. Only with a well organized program is a machine owner able to monitor the conditions of his equipment, to predict production based on machine availability and to schedule repairs and overhaul in advance. Analysis of accurately compiled maintenance records supplies him virtually all information needed for performance evaluation, repair or replacement decision, and cost-of-operation reviews. There is no single preventive maintenance program that fits every job, and there is no single way to do the job. New ideas, equipments and methods are introduced continually. The goal is the same i.e elimination of premature equipment failure by means of complete field maintenance. Preventive maintenance programs of any scope require teamwork and a master plan. Each equipment application in the field will require modifications of this form to match the working conditions, size of operation, and type of equipment. Every phase of a preventive maintenance program must be carefully planned, necessary reporting forms prepared, and each assignment clearly defined. Today more complex and productive construction equipment requires a well organized preventive maintenance program. Complete records are especially important. With costs for each machine recorded, guesswork and personal opinion have given away to factual cost analysis. More equipment owners are realizing that preventive maintenance is much more important than machine repair to increase the machines functional ability and increase or keep on operating it for years. Yet preventive maintenance is an investment that must be managed and controlled. Hiring a preventive maintenance specialist is a practical way to solve the problem or purchase the services. In case of the owners permanent service capability efficiency and cost of a service facility are greatly affected by location. The place must be accessible for employees and suppliers. Proper transportation connections are indispensable. The lot must accommodate all activities related to the operation. Its size is ten times the floor area of the building in order to accommodate employee, visitor and equipment parking, open-air storage and traffic access to all entrances. The land should be level and dry. The subsoil must support heavy loads. Natural hazards such as flooding and earth slides limit the usefulness of the facility. Obstructions like overhead cables, underground pipelines, ditches and gulleys should be avoided. Local building codes, zoning regulations and future highway plans should be investigated before the site is selected. The type of service work performed may require specialization areas within the service facility. These may include welding and metal fabrication, painting and sandblasting booths; track rebuild, electrical engine, and transmission shops; and tire repair and hydraulics repair areas. The total maintenance contract concept can be broadened to the point of fixing total equipment cost. This is a total cost contract under which the equipment dealer guarantees the owning cost of a machine for a specific time period. This contract may include provisions for the dealer to buy the machine back for a predetermined price when the contract ends. If an equipment owner is working in one particular area and machine applications remain relatively constant, the dealer might wish to extend the service to him. To ensure the lowest operating cost and to guarantee satisfactory performance, the dealer must retain a control of equipment maintenance.

With an adequate method of evaluating machine system performance and overall condition, it is possible to locate a wearing part, to monitor its gradual wear and to correct or replace it before major trouble arises. Today with the hydraulic testing units used by equipment dealers, such mistakes are rare. Test equipment is also used on engines and power shift transmissions. When used by experienced personnel, testing equipment can diagnose situations with astonishing ease, pinpoint particular service needs, and save costs in parts and repair time. To understand an equipment spread an owner should inspect every major piece of equipment regularly to determine its actual condition. Productivity differential is the cost of retaining a machine when an improved more productive model is available. It is not part of equipment cost except for comparison with a new machine and has the effect of adjusting the comparison of cost per hour to cost per unit of work accomplished. The productivity advantage offered by a new machine may be estimated using specification data and other information. Whenever predictable estimates should be verified through observed performance. An on-site demonstration can be requested of the equipment dealer, or machine performance can be observed at some other site. Productivity differential cost may either be added as a cost of the present equipment or subtracted from the cost of the new machine. It is an additive cost. As with downtime cost, the cost of productivity differential should not be considered if that extra productivity is not actually usable. Price increases due to inflation may be considered or may be ignored depending upon the intended usage of the equipment cost data. When the data are to be used for comparative purposes, constant dollar value may be assumed. Equipment managers should make cost estimates and prepare the cost schedules to reflect actual cost and usage experience.

Past experience of machine productivity is a major factor in determining the size machine will deliver the best productivity for the job. The buyers own experience can be supplemented, upon request, by that of the equipment dealer. Today, many dealers are equipped to provide data and counseling on machine capability under various operating conditions. Primary usage is an important consideration in determining size and choosing machine attachments. Efficient productivity in the primary usage should be given priority. Some compromise may be demanded in secondary usage. Operating conditions have a substantial effect on machine productivity. Wheel tractor-scrapers are for example more productive on a flat, straight, well-maintained haul road than they are on an uphill, winding rough road. They can be loaded faster with some materials than others. Some materials are difficult to eject and spread on the fill, whereas others dump clean and fast. All conditions of work cycle should be accounted for machine productivity.

A well financed company should stay away from leases except short term ones. Many leases end in ultimate acquisition either from the start of a lease on rental purchase basis or lease with purchase at fair market value. This is the most expensive form of acquiring equipment. Job conditions may change or a superintendant may decide that he must have his particular item beyond lease period. If this is not carefully policed, a contractor will pay for the equipment more than once including financing charges. Financial lease, operational lease, closed end leases and open end leases are the most talked about leases. Among them operational lease is for a period less than the normal life of the asset and therefore the commitment is less than the purchase price of the asset. In this type of arrangement the lessor will perform some sort of service in addition to routine maintenance i.e furnishing the asset.

With the profit increasing of the contractors organization, a purchasing personnel work closely with engineering personnel at the headquarters, regional and project levels to determine specific contract requirements to be purchased and subcontracts to be placed. They would normally review certain awards with engineering prior to placement to assure completeness of bills of material and adequacy of specifications and technical write-up. It furnishes with information, catalog and specification data relating to new or changed design equipment and new or improved materials, techniques, or procedures of which it may not be aware. When requested the purchasing department contacts the logical manufacturing or supply sources for pricing information or data required by engineering personnel. Purchasing personnel make enquiries to save engineering time for the initial contact and for the sales follow up which in addition to being time consuming is unnecessary at this point. The reason for restricting contacts from vendors is that, the source to be contacted will be determined with subsequent pricing in mind should the enquiry ever result in purchase. The contractor operating on a national or international basis, cannot possibly stuff each job with procurement specialists for the many varied categories of materials, equipment, subcontracts and services that must be provided. Thus the procurement specialists must of necessity be concentrated in company headquarters and will normally, in complete cooperation with divisional and project management and engineering, place the major orders for materials going into the construction, the major sub-contracts and all items of high dollar value. Contract type items will usually include such items as tires, fuels, oils and lubricants, high quality cement, aggregates and similar items that can be purchased to best advantage by the most experienced buyers available to the home office purchasing department. Almost invariably major equipment purchases are effected at the central headquarters purchasing department by staff personnel knowledgeable in the types of equipment under procurement and with the specification guidance from equipment specialists at the contractors equipment division. Projects particularly those that are large, will be staffed with a project or field purchasing agent to handle the purchase of miscellaneous operating supplies, spare parts, and other parts not feasible for centralized headquarters procurement. The project purchasing agent will also be responsible for the issuance, on a timely basis, of delivery orders or releases against purchase orders or contracts placed by the central headquarters purchasing department. The project purchasing agent also has the responsibility for expediting deliveries and performance under all purchases and contracts for the project, regardless of whether centrally ordered or job ordered. On very large projects involving many individual purchases of complex or engineered items and numerous sub-contracts for phases of the work, it will be advantageous to staff the project engineering section with a materials engineer. The materials engineer will make certain that the purchase orders and subcontracts are placed to cover all items of materials and work required by project plans and specifications and will coordinate the overall expediting activity to assure subcontractor and materials availability on hand precisely when needed. For domestic operations the percentage of centralized buying at the contractor's headquarters as compared to the percentage of decentralized purchasing at job site will vary considerably even for similar projects. It will depend on a number of factors, such as size and type of job; its proximity to the contractor's home office; complexity, variety, quantities and dollar value of materials required; number of major subcontracts to be placed; strength or caliber of project for divisional management and local relationships. Inventory and availability of major equipment is normally maintained at the central headquarters purchasing departments. The control records will be kept either manually in the purchasing department or more often at larger companies in the electronic data processing centre. The equipment is allocated to the contractor's various operating divisions according to their individual needs. Each division controls and is responsible for the equipment assigned to it, within the contractors established policies for usage rates, depreciation, overhaul and repair and time worked. During the course of the contract work, accurately and up-to-date records of progress should be kept currently. They should show in some computerized, diagrammatic or graphical way how actual progress compares with original progress estimates. Project management thus can see at a glance if the work is on schedule and that the allowable contract time will be met, if it is behind schedule and subject to late completion and financial penalties subject to late completion are specified or if early completion with savings in costs is possible. Early completion invariably results in savings due to improved production and in lesser overhead costs over the shorter construction period. Alert people constantly strive to complete work ahead of schedule, if overall cost do not result. Periodic programming is essential for controlling future activities. Many construction contracts require programming as monthly or quarterly intervals with the frequency depending on the kind and complexity of work involved. In this connection it is important that all interested parties be kept informed of the current program, that subcontractors agree to all changes, that material and equipment deliveries be rescheduled and reordered accordingly. The construction industry has possibly been one of the last segments to adopt scientific controls for better planning and coordination of operations. This might be because of the nature of the construction, in which organizations are formed and disbanded for each job, and because unique problems exist at practically every construction site. Construction projects are of shorter duration than manufacturing, mining and other continuing activities, and thus are less adaptable to minute control. With the advent of CPM and PERT a finer degree of programming has become more feasible. If the activity is computerized it permits rapid reprogramming, which reflects the effect on subsequent operations and reestablishes the critical sequence through the contract execution. Preliminary and basic scheduling of the work is mandatory to establish a concept of methods and operations for its performance within the allowable or a reasonable period of time, regardless of the system of programming chosen. The graph although limited in reflecting greatly refined programming without the excessive use of engineering manpower can work throughout the life of the contract to show the general status of the work items or subdivisions of work.

    Contacts and negotiations with vendors can be handled through a competent purchasing department personnel. They can make preliminary summary analyses of quotations and conditions applying thereto, passing them on to the estimated group. The latter should review the purchasing department's findings to ensure compliance with the contract specifications and to verify the proposed delivery dates will meet the proposed construction program. At the pre-bid stages direct communication between prospective subcontractors and the estimating staff is important, since a detailed mutual study of the tender documents is very necessary. Prospective subcontractors should be instructed to submit written proposals in advance of the bid date, quoting in compliance with the tender documents, stating the times of their intended performance and suggesting in advance the special condition on which pricing is based. Material and subcontract prices should be tabulated and summarized with respect to work items or subsection of the tender document to which they apply so that they can be readily compared. Unless the shortage of time prevents considering such proposals, they must be evaluated for the conditions, but leaving the pricing blank to be filled in nature and incorporating the overall proposal for the project. Construction market is getting highly competitive and with the ever increasing cost of machinery, labor, and materials, the successful contractor must use the most economical method available to accomplish the work. The engineer is responsible to keep up with the construction machinery which provides greater efficiency at lower cost. Every job therefore requires the contractor to choose one of a number of possible solutions and devise something new for the particular situation. To the extent that time permits, cost and method studies should be applied when the pre-bid estimate for a job is prepared so that the apparently chosen feasible method of construction can be selected as a basis for the proposal. After a successful tender has been placed and more time is available, a complete review of the methods and cost of accomplishing the work should be completed before investments in plant and equipment are made, and before personnel and facilities are moved to the site. If proper plant equipment and methods are being chosen, the postbid period may reconsider sub contracting parts of the work. It is important to reevaluate the effectiveness of the methods being used. The engineer should look at providing greater efficiency and thus lower the ultimate cost. The basic concept for plant and equipment should remain the same, but in subsidiary operations there should be concrete forming, the use of new devices for compaction of incidental fills and the better blast hole for rock excavations can result in substantial savings. Continuous processes present the greatest possibility of large production and substantial savings. A wheel-type excavator digging from a bank or stockpile and loading the output on a conveyor system which carried the material on a continuous flow to its final position or temporary surge pile not requiring intermittent handling.

Taking into account the estimating manual, it should do the following: serve as an indispensable check list and guide to estimating engineers making site investigations and accumulating basic data for prospective work. Assist in the training of estimating engineers and minimize the effort necessary to supervise the preparation of estimates and to relate them to basic data from the files. It is important to set up a step by step procedure for estimating to establish a sequence and format that can be easily read and followed by other company estimators. Direct the estimator in the proper breakdown of costs to parallel the established company accounting system thus allowing a direct comparison of the costs reported later during construction. Direct the project engineers and others in the preparation of company estimates and cost reports. Assist in summarizing various parts of the estimates into their various elements for analysis and comparison with other estimates that assist in establishing the cost accounting breakdown for new work for the benefit of all concerned. Heavy construction often is remotely situated. It is usually handled by contractors who do not normally operate in the area. They are at some distance from materials, facilities and labor. Local vendors, purveyors of services and supplies and the labor market and its leaders, often begins with and ends with each project. The shorter the job more difficult it is to organize greater efficiencies into the operations. An efficient work force of adequate size is a substantial one. Construction methods and machines used on building projects are standardized to a greater degree than for heavy construction. The machines are generally of smaller capacity and less complex. The work is more ordinary than other constructions and highly repetitive. Experienced specialists and specialized devices are readily available. Almost invariably there is a great difference in the cost of concrete forms for building and heavy construction. Concrete sections are generally less massive for buildings, concrete placing rates are slower and goes with less impacts than heavy work. Some of the formed concrete surfaces like exterior materials are to be covered, such as masonry, plaster and prebuilt panels, tolerances, surface finish. This permits less sophisticated form construction and less effort for their alignment. The most economical construction methods and procedures is by providing a solution that considers contract compliance, time of performance, productivity and efficiency. All the bidders are not necessarily on the same footing except for contract compliance. Control of patented devices, existing ownership, immediate availability of construction facilities, the techniques of specially trained help can favor one bidder to another. Construction of construction methods and their application must start with the factors that the contractor's experience has shown to be satisfactory and workable. The basic rules of selecting construction methods are through the following: staying with known principles on which historical cost experience is available, except that new devices or procedures may be considered if they use known principles with proven background for which accurate costs can be estimated in correlation with other uses. If the construction procedure cannot perform work don't attempt to price it. Price the work on sure methods and procedures and adapt or develop cost cutting possibilities during the performance of the contract. It is important to hire reliable experts to price and perform specialized or unfamiliar work.

To facilitate the estimating, particularly on large, heavy construction projects, it is often desirable and necessary to make preliminary layouts and design of various construction facilities expected to be used. For some projects the location and access to job buildings and shops are important features to indicate on maps. This makes it important to understand how they serve the various sections of work, principal roads and haul roads often have to be designed for location, line and grade. Temporary bridges must be sketched to show construction details and weight limits. Excavating and grading for plant sites, cableway runways etc require detailing. How the various craning and handling facilities would reach the different sections of the work often must be illustrated. Plant foundations and supporting structures should be sketched up sufficiently to permit preliminary designs. Scheduling of the construction operations is an inseparable part of the estimating function. If possible the construction time might be shortened compared with that allowed in the tender documents. Ultimate cost savings then might be realized as a result of reducing such continuing obligations as overhead. This is definitely desirable to project financing plans that permits earlier payments under the contract.

Some construction plant facilities are very complex and highly technical. They must be designed sufficiently ahead of the original estimating to ensure reasonably accurate pricing that will cover the ultimate cost of providing and constructing the facilities if the tender is successful. In the case of whirley crane trestles, the sizes of structural members, length of trestle, legs to fit the terrain, cross bracing, crane and railroad track layouts must be calculated and known and stretched out for the record. To provide coverage of proposed permanent structure they should determine the character and amount of runway excavations, the structural design of towers and backstay systems.

Few construction operations vary so widely in cost and character as forms for concrete, and few involve in larger labor factor than wood forms. Labor productivity has a marked influence on the cost of forms; therefore every effort should be made to engineer them in advance. Steel forms usually provide these features, but their costs and initial assembly is relatively expensive. Wood forms should be designed well ahead of time and drawings prepared for their assembly and erection. In the case of cost for new pricing if such adjusted pricing of concrete forms is not used for the initial pricing, it should be used to verify the estimated cost through other means. Since forms comprise the largest part of the cost of most concrete jobs and there is a high labor factor, the possibility of inaccurate pricing is greater than virtually any other construction operation.

A generalized cost estimate for a project consists of the percentage completion curve showing forecasted and actual cumulative percent completion plotted on a time scale and used primarily as a control tool. labor schedules developed for separate classifications of labor and showing the number of men required each time period. Equipment schedules developed for separate types and size of equipment and showing the number of units required each time period. Another important element to deal with is material schedules for important items of material or installed equipment indicating deadlines for such steps as preparation of shop drawings, approval of drawings of samples, beginning of fabrication, date of shipment and date needed at job site. Financial schedules indicating on a time scale, the cumulative income received to date, the cumulative expenses to date and the differences between the two to show the amount of financing required during each time period. There are many activities for example the bar chart of a concrete dam project might show a single bar representing earth excavation that extended across the entire project duration. It was accurate since earthwork operations were in progress every month of the job span. The network techniques require a level of breakdown such that every activity must be completed before a following one commences. The earthwork activity would have to be broken down into many additional activities representing excavation for various purposes such as abutments, Stage I dam foundation; Stage II, powerhouse substructure, tailrace, core trench, canal intake. Items such as the procurement of important materials, preparations, and approval of drawings and designs and obtaining permits are seldom shown on a bar chart. To understand a network model the normal procedure of developing an overall network diagram, complete scheduling data and supplementary reports and schedules that are of value. Use the dateline cutoff method of sub-networking covering the span of the first month and overlapping at least a week into the second month. Whenever changes occur during the month, incorporate them into the subnet and manually make forward pass computations only. This is practical since, regardless of the size of the project network, the subnet should be relatively small and only forward pass computations should be involved. The critical path can be easily identified by backtracking from the final node of the revised subnet. Additional information regarding revised float times could be obtained by the added effort of making backward pass calculations in the subnet, but this is not essential.

A simple procedure is briefly outlined as a basis of discussing and understanding some of the features of resource allocation methods by setting availability limits for each resource type. These may be definite cut offs that cannot be exceeded, or there may be a range of units above the normal limits that involve a premium cost. By progressively lowering the limits set, the procedure being described can be used for resource leveling purposes. At the beginning of the project all activities should be considered that are available for scheduling. It is important to schedule the activity having the highest priority. The principal variations in different procedures involves the basis used for determining the priorities of the activities available for scheduling. There must be sufficient levels of priority rules established that a decision is reached in every situation. For example, primary priority might be given to the activity available for scheduling which has the lowest latest start date on the basis that if an activity is scheduled later than its latest start date, it will delay project completion. If two or more activities have the same latest start date, secondary priority might be given to the activity whose updated earliest start date occurred latest which would be equivalent to selecting the most nearly critical of the activities. If two or more activities are still eligible, a third degree of priority might be established based on the order of activity listing. Project duration may increase during the process since the start time of some activities may have to be delayed beyond their latest start dates. An ideal resource allocation procedure would combine the strong points of both approaches. It would take advantage of the power of the computer to store and manipulate information and to make rapid computations for resource schedules. They should identify critical activities, scheduling and float data, and dynamic updating as rescheduling was performed. Remote consoles in the contractor's field office communicating with large, timesharing central computers permit the development of interactive procedures that can combine the strong points described above. Some times cost trade-off possibilities involve resource scheduling changes. The addition of an extra unit of a resource type permits a new set of resource schedules to be developed that may result in a reduced project duration. The reduction in duration provides a cost slope for this possible change. The availability of idle resources offers opportunities for time cost trade-offs at reduced cost slopes. The extra resource units may be used to shorten such activity durations with little or no increase in cost. Scarce resource types often result in project schedule and does not have a critical path. Project duration is partly determined by activities that have been postponed due to lack of sufficient resource units.

One of the most difficult things to compute accurately is often the most significant item in a project-transportation of earth. This is becoming more difficult to compute because of the extreme size of the transporting units presently employed. Many of these are in the 150 ton gross weight category four or five times heavier than a maximum size highway truck. It is extremely difficult to calculate properly the momentum and inertia for these. Also with new torque converter drives, it is difficult to calculate the acceleration time of such units from starting or for any significant grade change. Almost all of the major equipment manufacturers of transporting units have developed computer programs to calculate the performance of their products under varying conditions of grade. The individual units capability are installed in the computer employing the published performance data, generally to include grade ability, speed, rim pull. The fuels, net and gross, and weights are also part of the required data. Many times speed limitations will have to be considered because the estimator knows that the road has many curves which will limit speed.

Data processing systems and techniques in the construction industry have been firmly established over the last few years. Present data processing users are found in all segments of the industry, and the areas of application are broad. The environment today is one of expanding application, extending from the mechanization of such functions as payroll, cost, and scheduling to the mechanization of certain parts of the estimating operation. Data processing systems are being used for the planning and scheduling of projects and for the control of project costs through responsive cost control systems. Several factors have resulted in this growing mechanization of the estimating function. First, companies using data processing systems in cost capturing functions are accumulating data for estimating which can be used automatically. Proper coding of cost data allows much of the information to have applications on subsequent bids. Mechanization relieves the estimator of the clerical functions of looking up standards and performing calculations, and allows more time to be spent on the important aspect of determining the method of construction. Data processing permits the user in the construction industry to make minor or major changes to estimates and to be aware of the changes in relatively short time. The only manual processing is the preparation of records which reflects the proposed changes. These records are then inserted in the estimate file and the old records pulled out, this is the starting of the automated process. Contractors that have mechanized estimating functions are further provided the facility to evaluate quickly the effect of alternative proposals. Alternative proposals could represent different methods of construction, more than one type of equipment, or more than one type of material. In a proposal related to schedule preparation the overall project should be broken down into the items of work which should be independently scheduled. This operation may be performed in the estimating cycle. A unique code number may be assigned to each activity, which conforms to the numbering conventions of the particular scheduling system employed. Cost control in the construction industry encompasses the gathering of cost data by some predetermined classification, the relating of actual costs to estimated costs, and the reporting to management and current of current cost status as effective cost control system have two main prerequisites. An efficient cost-keeping function can point out to management, not only which costs are high, but also why the costs are over the budget. When estimates of labor costs have been made in detail by craft, analysis of costs incurred can point out which crafts are performing unsatisfactorily compared to the estimate. Effective cost control can inform management of high costs because of excessive downtime and repair charges for a certain type of equipment. Once the project budget has been determined and set up at the cost-code level, the project personnel are concerned only with the cost codes applicable to the particular job. In general two viewpoints prevail among data processing in construction which cover the use of captured labor performance standards. The first involves the use of standards in an automated estimating system i.e applying labor standards to the estimated quantity of each cost item. Another part is retrieval of past labor costs to be used for information purposes for estimating. From a data processing standpoint maintenance of performance records represents a valuable by product of the cost control system.

Cost keeping for construction equipment, particularly in heavy construction, constitutes an important application area for data processing system. In recent years tremendous increases in productivity of construction equipment have been noted. The technological improvements have been accompanied by increases in the cost of the equipment, and as a result, ownership of equipment constitutes a substantial part of the assets of many contractors. The need for effective control of equipment costs parallels the need for control of labor costs. One method incorporates the charging of all equipment costs to a single cost code. Many construction companies have emphasized development of systems to maintain equipment records on their data processing systems. The equipment record keeping application includes such functions as recording of depreciation, scheduling of preventive maintenance, recording of maintenance charges and fuel consumption and analysis of rates. Entries to systems are provided by purchase orders for new equipment, equipment cost/time cards and shop-work orders for maintenance.

To look forward towards the accounting for equipment costs the accumulation of historical cost data which can serve as a basis for estimating costs, making repair or replace decisions and comparing costs on different makes of comparable equipment. Costs may be segregated into two categories those incurred as a result of having the equipment available for use and those incurred as a result of operating the equipment. Ownership costs cover such items as depreciation, rental, taxes, licenses etc. Certain decisions are made regarding the operation of equipment like: whether labor costs related to operators of rolling stock should be charged to project costs or operating costs on the equipment. The labor believes that such costs should be charged on the project rather than on the equipment. A decision must be reached as to whether the project or the equipment should be charged for fuel costs related to operation of equipment. One procedure involves charging line item cost for operating costs on the equipment at a rate which includes a predetermined per hour for fuel costs with an offsetting credit to job overhead equal to the fuel cost factor. Equipment repairs can be classified into two different types, those done at repair facilities and those done at the project site. Cost applicable to the maintenance of equipment repair facilities and labor applicable thereto should be distributed to the units on the basis of job orders. They enter into determination of hourly rate covering operating costs on the equipment. It is possible to have an exception to this procedure by charging the cost of repairing wrecked equipment in excess of any insurance recovery to project costs.

The effect of the inflationary cycle in the construction industry has been felt at the bargaining table by industrial leaders. Industrial unions are pointing to the collective bargaining gains made by the building and construction tradesmen and are using these settlements to formulate their demands with the industrial owners. Heretofore, the industrial owner has purchased the services from the construction owner fully recognizing that it was to his advantage economically to do so. The skill capabilities of the construction worker under the direction of the construction contractor under the competitive bid as the negotiated bid system provided him with a service and purchasing of a facility at a cost than he himself could accomplish. The government has been studying the method of awarding contracts, which causes most of the construction activities to be concentrated in a seasonal period and often results in an erroneous and unnecessary shortage of craftsmen. With all of the problems relating to increasing costs and the recognition of concern on the part of the purchasers of construction services and facilities, contractor groups are trying to improve all aspects of the outlook for the industry. Problems arise due to slowing down the rate of wage costs. The include slowing down the demands that the industry has faced. Contractor groups may contribute to a slowing down process through better preparation and stronger positions at the bargaining table. More unification and association between various segments of the contractors association might be able to accomplish more effective negotiation. Funding policy, accounting, insurance, taxes, legal and contractual problems are some of the other abilities and demands and necessities that contractors should have.

Chapter 8

Essentials of total quality management and beyond it

(BY BAISHAM CHATTERJEE)

TQM has been continuously changing from its applications, to concepts to its different stages. Implementing TQM of a very high standard is mainly in the case of low performers that need to concentrate on the fundamentals. Low performers need to concentrate on the fundamentals of TQM-building the organizations capacity to develop and deliver reliable products and services. This is possible by building the human resource infrastructure, listening to customers to get better at what they already do, and redesigning business processes. In high performing companies some of the highly touted practices, such as benchmarking, employee empowerment and externally oriented planning tools. Focusing on the emerging paradigm and the broader systems, it may be unending, proactive to opportunities and big breakthroughs and small steps that create the first step to TQM. Learning modern benefits, openness, seek process or system fix and management is responsible. There are many advantages of TQM. The first is that it gets managers to attend to internal results and processes. Zero defects and no rework efficiency distract people from adding value and excitement to customers life. Taking into view the quality of design and redesign: product designs conform to customer needs like automobile car seats after which comes quality of conformance that says all similar products for same use all for a particular purpose should have similar designs. All these customer improvement processes improve customer value. Marketing people tend to have a user based and product based view that focuses on matching product characteristics with customer perception. Quality of conformance is a secondary issue, after they have seen that design to customer needs. Thus managers in the new paradigm regard quality as an important element to strategy formulation and planning: deciding which markets to enter, which products to offer, which customers to serve, and how to outperform competitors. Fulfilling the responsibility for systems and processes ensures that managers take action to reduce variation and achieve continuous improvement. Top managers are responsible for designing for quality by making quality planning a part of business planning. Quality goals or quality improvement projects should be deployed down through the hierarchy by breaking them into sub-goals at lower levels and in this top managers should form quality councils that establish and oversee project teams to improve macro-processes.

Company-wide quality control goes beyond TQC where the policy deployment cascades improvement targets and links means and ends throughout every function and level of the organization. The cross-functional goals of QCS (Quality, cost and scheduling) are clearly defined as superior to such line functions as design, production and marketing. To go beyond TQM implies that managers should not do quality by implementing programs. In many organizations, managers regard TQM as a sideline activity, a corporate program which requires only a few hours each week. The definition of TQM developed by the working committee of the Total Quality Forum dispelled this misconception by separating the underlying principles from the tools and techniques that are often used to apply the principles. In a transitional period, with some organizations or industries experiencing anomalies and just now sensing the need for change, and with some organizations or industries making the paradigm shift. Certainly the contrast of the old paradigm versus the new, emerging paradigm represents extremes, and most organizations fall somewhere in the middle ground and shifting to a new paradigm will mean different things for different organizations. This may simply have to rearrange and integrate some of the diverse elements or quality programs into an integrated whole, or develop new cultural values and beliefs to support the new paradigm. TQM set product quality improvements to reduce defect levels to less than 100 parts per million and achieve 100 percent customer satisfaction. They have statistical process control, and quality improvement and problem-solving techniques. The maintenance department uses statistical charting to monitor the downtime of machines in the production department. In the new paradigm shift just implementing the use of a new technique or tool, or redefining employee roles does constitute a paradigm a little bit. The modern control and improvement process of the emerging paradigm, incorporates some of the elements of the traditional control process along with the statistical approach to the study of variation and its causes. The modern control and improvement process is built around four basic building blocks that very simply describe the process of performance. These building blocks are input, transformation, output and customer value. Before the transformation process can occur, however various inputs have to be prepared. The strategy, structure, product designs, machinery, plant layout, policies, procedures for work, rules for conduct, materials, human resources all have to be put in place before anything can be done to transform inputs into outputs for customers. Traditional product specifications often tolerate a range of variation around a target, whereas an emphasis on continuous improvement encourages the reduction of variation around a target. Application of the measure-study-act sequence can be divided in 4 types: preliminary control of inputs, concurrent control of the transformation process, rework control, damage control to smooth relations with customers. Continuously executing a customer value strategy creates a challenge: continuous improvement requires change, but consistent customer value requires stability. Breakthrough means a big improvement is accomplished through radical departure from past practices. A breakthrough may come through creativity, when an old system is disregarded or scrapped. Creators synthesize and develop ideal systems with a clean slate. Most managerial breakthroughs are the result of innovation. In innovation, existing technologies, processes, or components of existing systems are recombined or re-assimilated in novel ways. The innovated system as a whole fundamentally differs from that which existed before. Examples are like Sony's product innovation incorporating computer technology and a microphone to produce filmless camera that offers a soundtrack to accompany each frame. The camera records images on a reusable floppy disk that can be played back instantly on any television set. This combination of existing technologies resulted in a superior means of quickly recording, re-experiencing, and sharing memorable images. After this process comes incrementalism where small improvements are accomplished. It may result from creativity or innovation; however it most often results when existing systems are adjusted and modified by slight alterations. The accumulation of a number of relatively small incremental improvements can have a tremendous impact. Hughes aircraft showed their idea of incremental innovation by building satellites in a more cost effective manner. They began by mapping out every step from design to delivery. Working in design, manufacturing, purchasing and marketing they identified 131 steps that were candidates for improvement. By making small changes like moving a hole quarter of an inch so an inspector could insert a testing probe more easily, Hughes cut the time it took to build a satellite control processor—the brains of the machine-from 45 weeks to 22 weeks. This saved millions of dollars but this does not happen until proposed changes are put in place.

Standardization means imposed standards such as specifications, protocols, rules, and procedures for the uniformity of materials, parts, products, machines, dies, tools etc. Standards are an important part of standardization and managers verify the operability and performance new systems before releasing them to use. It also involves transmitting information about the systems purpose and architecture, to educate people who work with the system and demonstrate that the system work is intended. They display strategic focus, statistical capability, and predictability for stable on-target system performance. Defects through standardization add costs to the product in the form of rework, inspection hours, lost capacity and lower customer value. In routinization, systems are balanced, fine-tuned and mastered by subordinates responsible for mastering the system. The benefits of rountinization are through the learning curve that shapes behavior through successive approximation. Not only does this imply an expectation for smoother and more accurate performance with each repetition it also implies repetition at appropriate times. All these and the power of knowledge cannot be harnessed without the second component of technology: tools. Tools include, instruments, machines, algorithms, programs and are used to do the work that produces valued good and services.

Operational tasks may be broken down into component motions such as observable, physical, behavioral movements and unobservable mental movements. The work of technological tools, for computers and automated machine tools, may be considered in operational motions. Operating methods are the ways of using the available technology, that is knowledge and tools, and other assets to do the work of the strategic systems. Operating methods include the standard rules, procedures, protocols, and arrangement of tasks through which individuals measure work. Operating methods are critical in providing customer value, because they determine whether process technology and material, mechanical and human assets are formally utilized. Higher benefits are relative to sacrifices, the higher will be the value. Managers can increase the customer value of a product by increasing the benefits or decreasing the sacrifices. To make improvements that strategically enhance customer value, managers need measurement systems to help them determine what customers value and assess the delivery of customer value. The measurement system should span the customers perception of means and ends relationship, use processes, value delivered, and satisfaction and dissatisfaction. Armed with the knowledge, managers can design and deliver products of the best value. To develop such a measurement system, managers must understand all of the components of the means/ ends model. Needs vary from one individual to the next, and so the anticipated value of a product may be very idiosyncratic or particular to each individual customer. People with similar needs derive similar value from the product and a product might be useful to one and useless to some other. For this a marketing person should understand the different customer groups and how a market is segmented. Top executives and middle managers make most of the key decision about overall direction and allocate resources to achieve the key goals. This business unit must identify and satisfy market needs effectively and efficiently by formulating their own strategies and organization goals, building capability and integrating their efforts. Functional and department level managers and employees must implement the business strategies efficiently. International research on quality practices indicates that explaining the strategic plan to employees, customers and suppliers; improving and simplifying production and development processes; and shortening cycle times consistently benefit every organization. The product market hierarchy defines the structure of the managers. Starting from the basic customer need underlying the opportunity like monitoring, a market hierarchy breaks down a generic class of products or services into specific product types, which are further into the various brands that are direct competitors within each product type. Managers must avoid defining the product-market hierarchy and market segments with general demographic or technology variables until after the market has been segmented on benefits the customers want or the customers situation. If segments do not differ on at least one of the behaviors, on the benefits customers seek, or in the situations they use the product, then the segments are not different in a way useful to the firm. Developing a company-wide understanding of the sacrifices that customer must make to use the product also improves customer orientation. Clear values, focused vision, and sustainable core competences must be exciting and bold enough to change the way employees think about the organization from a production focus to customer service perspective. Many firms have dramatically reduced the number of suppliers to as few as one for each part. Although this makes the firm more dependant on its suppliers, it helps improve incoming quality, minimize inventory costs, and put in just-in-time systems into place. This raises output, productivity, quality and customer value. The performance measure is essential for evaluating how well one is meeting customer needs. Improving financial performance and growth are good signs, but either can also disguise declining share. To evaluate any internal performance against customer expectations, managers must use direct measures from the market and managers should be market sensitive rather than financially sensitive. To evaluate firm performance, managers should understand surveys, product returns, customer calls, focus groups, order feedback forms, and customers alternative product applications with ratio analysis, market share and stock performance. Determining that function, activity and process analyses requires a thorough qualitative assessment of strategies, tactics and customer value, traditionally internal analysis focused on functional specification which means that it is limited to strengths and weaknesses within each function. While quality function deployment QFD focuses on cross-functional or horizontal integration, planning is highly participatory, vertical, top-down and bottom-up process used primarily as a coordinating or linking activity in the organization.

Many quality problems can be traced to overspecialization and the resulting sub-optimization by departments and functions. An organization's structure must resolve the inherent conflict between the need for specialization at the functional level and the need for integration across the business. Qualitative information should be collected in the earliest and latest stages of research to deepen understanding of how customers really think about the product in each situation. Open ended interviews, focus groups, and customer complaint data are particularly useful as sources of qualitative response. Both qualitative and quantitative data should be collected systematically to facilitate later analysis and interpretation. Similarly taking the case of customer value, advancing from abacus, to slide rule to calculator improves performance on these key characteristics that drive customer value and the electronic calculator provides much more accuracy. Technological change means such actions are insufficient to meet the customers real or changing needs. High-tech modern calculators can improve their production system, lower total costs and thus improve the value of slide rules. The best analysis is a QFD that provides a way to integrate and subordinate specialized functions and departments into coordinated, collaborative activity that provides customer value. While many organizations don't choose a structured technique like this, they write operational definitions and articulate the means of providing value to customers. The ideas would have to be translated into processes and operations to produce the product and services. QFD provides communication among specialized experts mainly to the manufacturing, marketing and engineering staff to do this work. The chief advantage of the QFD approach over other mechanisms is that it integrates at a system level, different departmental activities through common task requirements. This minimizes deviation from customer wants throughout the product design and production cycle. Companies that use QFD can achieve a competitive advantage by delivering the products and services customers want. QFD can eliminate warranty claims and help reduce developmental cost and time to market. QFD yielded several process improvements in product development, such as structuring and decision making process across functional groups, building a well organized highly motivated team for efficient transfer of information. QFD may improve long term process performance more than short term product gains. Each step of the process in the house of quality, design matrix, operating matrix, and control matrix is based on clearly defined measures that incorporate customer needs and values. With simultaneous consideration of customer needs, engineering capabilities, and process design, QFD can contribute continuous cross-functional participation from start to finish and generates consensus decisions about trade-offs. Processes are composed of four phenomena: processing, inspection, transport and delay. To improve a process, one cannot simply improve the machining operation, or the inspection operation or the transport operation, that are a part of the flow. Improving the overall process for better cycle time, would require a JIT approach that eliminates the need to transport batches of material from one machine group to another. After suppliers delivered components directly to the assembly process, the entire warehousing operation was found to be necessary. A system is composed of multiple and diverse kinds of processes, and the flow of work is not simply sequential, from one operation or process to another. A demanding approach to manufacturing, JIT requires shortened lead times, inventory minimization, equipment reliability, balanced flows and predictable performance throughout the system. Operation managers must focus on the overall system, and must stabilize or reduce variation in processes, eliminate unnecessary inventories, reduce the time to set up machines and do production changeovers. Purchasing must ensure that incoming materials are delivered on time, in the right quantity, and with consistent quality, rather than simply granting contracts to low bid suppliers to meet cost objectives. This is very different from simply working to maintain standards for scrap, rework, efficiencies and utilization of machinery. In the case of Cadillac Motor co, Cadillac managers reconceived their vehicle design/ redesign system and implemented what they call simultaneous engineering SE. In simultaneous engineering, functional activities are done simultaneously as much as possible, with all participants working as a team. Departments have to quickly translate customer needs into designs and engineering specifications that are manufacturable. Designs are translated into engineering specifications and designers and engineers work together as a team on the new model that has been brought to the marketplace and it reduces development time, improves product quality, reduces costs and enhances customer value. The consumer experiences the effects of variation in products in the form of errors, delays, poor performance, reduced reliability, unpredictable delivery, lack of availability, and lack of uniformity, but everything depends on the frequency of purchase and use. In the repetitive production of units or repeated activities of internal processes this is easily calculated.

The effects of variation in demand on equipment capacity requirements must also be understood and accounted for in system design. Choice of equipment design affects skill requirements for employees, and so staffing decisions and equipment design decisions are interdependent. Intelligent selection of a particular system design involves predicting how variation in requirements placed on the capacity of a system of production or service will affect cost, quality and timeliness of delivery. It cant control performance but it can predict future events and go along with predictions. Variations can be done in undesirable, unanticipated form, standards were met, but other dimensions of performance, such as inventory cost were unfavorably affected, standards for accounting control and statistical control have to be met. The kind of control charts to be used in a given situation depends upon the kind of data to be examined, although specific details of construction may vary from one type of the chart to the next and are common to all control charts. A control chart with no points outside statistical control limits and no systematic patterns in the plotted points shows variation in statistical control. Statistical control limits are based on the data plotted on the chart. Reduced manufacturing effectiveness leads to increased costs, which are translated into either lowered profitability or increased prices, and a damaged competitive position. But the variation in dimension, given that assembly could be carried out, also shows up in product performance. Variation can lead to friction and wear, resulting in reduced reliability and impaired performance.

Production personnel carried out intensive studies of a coolant system, corrected a number of problems and studied and improved coolant properties. Process engineers worked with operators to determine the appropriate settings for feed rates and speeds, and standard operating systems were established. Assembly problems and scarp levels were reduced by the reduction in variation achieved, and a support of the plant management for the project. There is necessity for the position of a control engineer who knows control algorithm. Process engineers and control engineers can arrive at a tool adjustment algorithm that would not add to variation, while maintaining the target dimension. Restricting quality improvement work to processes at lower levels of an organization, such as production or assembly processes or service delivery processes, guarantees that the kinds of improvements achieved will be limited and will contribute little to the long-term effectiveness and survival of the enterprise.

Wide fluctuations in demand for manufactured products pose the dilemma for equipment capacity; either capacity is put into place to meet high demand levels, or inventory is built up during times of low demand to buffer against insufficient capacity during high demand periods. Equipment should stand idle during times of low demand; additional inventory and storage costs should be incurred. Meeting maximum levels of demand results in underutilization of equipment during periods of low demand; having equipment sufficient to meet only low to medium demand levels implies that sales will be lost during times when demand exceeds capacity. A division of an automobile company has reorganized its manufacturing operations into product teams and use cross-functional teams to jointly manage all of the activities involved in designing, producing the product and managing the work force. The responsibilities of design engineers have been increased to include introduction of their products in the production system. Design engineers work in production until good quality product is being produced at normal production volumes. The return to their design activities with improved knowledge of design factors affects the company's ability to manufacture the product. A team of engineers, production managers, and production operators works with major suppliers on improvement of incoming supplies. The initial production schedule for the customers next order will call for production of the number of assemblies that were produced to fill the previous order with less finished goods inventory on hand. Orders to suppliers will authorize shipment of enough material to produce the initially scheduled build, and additional materials will be expedited, if required. This policy is not optimal but it provides a means to show the effects of variation in product quality on some other dimensions of performance. There are numerous costs linked to and affected by production quality. Among them are costs for material handling, inspection, space, energy, overtime and supervision.

The complexity of continuous quality improvement in an organization like St Mary's is a lot different than in a widgets shop where someone is turning out little widgets, where someone can weigh them measure them and test them, the outcome measurement is something difficult. Understanding the processes is what we are getting better about and is beneficial for a lot of areas. The executives of the healthcare firm St Mary's are convinced that the improvement of quality has a direct and measurable effect on their costs of doing business. They believe that improving service quality for all customers and reducing costs will help them fulfill St Mary's mission. It requires both a framework for CQI and executive commitment for this kind of success. The executives need around 6 to 9 months time to make everybody know about CQI and themselves understanding the implementation and processes of CQI. A strong CQI effort will make a substantial contribution toward positioning, St Mary's as a preferential practice location for area physicians. The installation of CQI at St Mary's was designed to take place in six phases: decision phase, organization phase, preparation phase, initial implementation phase, expansion phase, and integration and sustaining phase. In a different way the delivery quality task force of Toyota split into two delivery quality working groups, each charged to formulate a comprehensive company-wide plan to improve vehicle delivery focused on the logistics through port processing and transportation. Toyota devotes much time, energy, and money to study teams, which exists at all levels of Toyota, in production plants and in corporate departments. The composition of the teams varies according to the nature of the issue, including chief engineers, manufacturing liaisons, production personnel or suppliers. The key elements of kaizen emphasize making sure that there is a good manufacturing system in place which is focused on optimizing overall flows and responding to customer demand. Another important part of kaizen is making tasks simpler and easier to perform, removing wasted motion, increasing the efficiency of the work process, maintaining a safe work environment and constantly improving the product quality. One of the features of the Toyota Production System is that it uses an approach called leveled production. TMM gets orders of monthly sales from TMS for all combinations of model types, colors and options. TMM divides those into a daily production plan and distributes them across the day so that the total number produced equals the daily plan. Leveled production shortens the lead time, or time it takes to respond to customer orders. The system is designed to produce vehicles in a sequence such that each is different from the one after it. Leveled production may give up a little of the cost advantages associated with the economies of scale available in mass production. TMM involves in-process inspection and does not wait until the finished gets to the end of the production line. The final inspection department takes each vehicle through a rigorous testing process involving thousands of inspectors throughout the testing facility. Through intensification of TQM principles and methods and the application of quality tools i.e competitive benchmarking, problem solving, root cause analysis. The voice of the customer will be heard and reflected in new products and services through the application of innovative technology and use of QFD to ensure that the design is in fact responsive to the customers requirements—as defined by the customer. The perspective that we have talked about is beyond TQM and the different basic concepts of TQM to make things easier are: a committed and involved management to provide long-term top to bottom organizational support. Internal and external unwavering focus on customer, effective involvement and utilization of the entire work force, treating suppliers as partners, establishing performance measures for processes and continuous improvement of the business and production process.

    The purpose of TQM is to provide a quality product or service to customers, increase productivity and lower cost. With a higher quality product and lower price, competitive position in the marketplace will be enhanced, this helps in achieving profit and growth with greater ease. The active involvement of middle managers and first line supervisors is essential to the success of the TQM effort. They are accountable for achieving many of the organization's performance goals and objectives, and they form enduring links in the communication chain from senior management to the front-line workers. Without middle managements early and active support, the TQM effort could fail. Senior management should ensure that managers at all levels have an opportunity, to develop ownership in the TQM effort and a chance to acquire the insights and skills necessary to become leaders. TQM implies an organizational obsession with meeting or exceeding customer expectations, so that customers are delighted. Understanding the customer's needs and expectations is essential to winning new business and keeping existing business. An organization must give its customers a quality product and service that meets their need at a reasonable price, which includes on-time delivery and outstanding service. To attain this level, the organization needs to continually examine their quality system to see if it is responsive to ever-changing customer requirements and expectations. One basic concept of TQM is an unwavering focus on customers, both internal and external. Most employees know about the external customer or end user but may not think of other employees as internal customers of their output. In the ideal organization, every employee would have direct contact with customers and be effective at meeting their needs. But the reality is that most employees are shielded from customers by organizational layers. One of the basic philosophy of TQM philosophy is continuous process improvement. This concept implies that there is an acceptable quality level because the customers needs, values and expectations are constantly changing and becoming more demanding. An organization can save both customers and money by training front-line employees to solve problems directly with customers. Customers want problems solved quickly and efficiently; therefore, employees should know to handle a wide range of situations that arise in customer relationship. Customer focus and listening skills are not easily learned. Recognition and reward should be linked to service quality performance and the ability to satisfy customers. In the case of focus groups imprint analysis is an emerging technique used. This is a good way to obtain the intrinsic feelings associated with a product or service. Feelings are not easily obtained from customer questionnaires, because customers often hold back information on surveys. Word association, discussion and relaxation techniques can identify a customers emerging needs even if the participants are not directly able to articulate those needs. Imprint analysis helps in understanding the human emotions involved in a purchase decision. Similarly quality control circles are groups of people from one work unit who voluntarily meet together on a regular basis to identify, analyze and solve quality and other problems within the area. They choose their own problems and focus on quality of work life and health safety issues rather than on improving work processes. They remain in existence over a long period, working on project after project. The members of a process improvement team represent each operation of the process or sub-process. Usually the scope of the teams activity is related to the work unit. During the course of the teams life additional expertise from other work areas may be added on a permanent or as needed temporary basis. The life cycle of the process improvement team is usually temporary-it is disbanded when the objective has been obtained. A design and review team is a good example of a cross-functional team.

As it indicates, a permanent process improvement team or a business improvement team that is directed by a quality council may address overall cross-functional improvements for the organization. By direction of the quality council, several cross-functional teams may be established to address specific improvement problems that span several functional areas. To expedite the forming stage, an individual should be tasked with chartering the team. In chartering a team, a facilitator commonly meets with the upper management to discuss the specific problem, then a macro flow-chart is developed involving the major process associated with the product, service or process. Performance appraisals may be for the teams or individuals. Regardless of the system, a key factor in a successful performance appraisal is employee involvement. An employee should get the opportunity to comment on the evaluation. Performance must be based on standards that are developed and agreed upon by the appraiser and employee. Performance appraisals should be viewed as a positive way to get employees involved. Appraisal is a tedious process but if the employee is interviewed very thoroughly before selection then tasks become easier and known to be performed by the newly recruited person. Appraisals nourish short-term performance and destroy long term planning. Frequently, long term gains are sacrificed by making the individual look good in the short term.

Process improvement begins with the establishment of an effective infrastructure such as quality council. Two of the duties of the council are to identify the improvement projects and establish the project teams with a project owner. The quality councils need to provide the teams with the resources to determine the causes, create solutions and establish controls to hold the gains. The problem solving method improves the processes, while the quality council is the driver that ensures that improvement is continuous and never ending. Reinvention is the most demanding improvement strategy. A new product, service, process or activity is developed using teams based on complete understanding of the customers requirement and expectations. In reinvention the team uses in-depth knowledge of the customers requirements and expectations and invents a new product, service, process or activity. There are three types of creativity: create new processes, combine different processes and modify the existing processes. Combining two or more processes is a synthesis activity to create a better process, and is a unique combination of what already exists and relies heavily on benchmarking. Areas for possible change are the number and length of delays, bottlenecks, equipment, timing and number of inspections, rework, cycle time and materials handling. In particular, reducing cycle times, lowering inventory levels, and searching for non-value-added activities are excellent sources for change, as these typically have many hidden costs that, if minimized or eliminated, affect a number of processes in the organization. Lowering inventory levels allows there to be less WIP to be transported, frees floor space, and lessens the management and accounting of the WIP, if the inventory is a time dated material.

The benefit of JIT is that inventory related costs are kept to a minimum. Procurement lots are small and delivery is frequent. As a result the supplier will have many more process setups, thus becoming a JIT organization itself. The supplier must drastically reduce setup time or its costs will increase. Because there is little or no inventory, the quality of incoming materials must be very good or the production line would be shut down. To be successful, JIT requires exceptional quality and reduced setup times. To make a supplier successful, the supplier should maintain high technological standards and has the capability of dealing with future technological innovations. The supplier can provide those raw materials and parts required by the purchaser, and those supplied meet the quality specifications. The supplier also should have the capability to produce the amount of production needed, or can attain the capability. Looking at the case of performance measures quality costs cross department lines by involving all activities of the organization, in this some costs such as inspector salaries and rework: are readily identifiable; other costs such as prevention costs associated with marketing, design and purchasing are more difficult to identify and allocate. Quality costs are used by management in its pursuit for quality improvement, customer satisfaction, market share and profit enhancement. It is the economic common denominator that forms the basic data for TQM. When quality costs are too high, it is a sign of management ineffectiveness, that can affect the organizations competitive position. A quality cost program provides warnings against dangerous, financial situations. A quality cost program quantifies the magnitude of the quality problem in the language that management knows best i.e dollars. The cost of poor quality can exceed 20% of sales dollars in manufacturing companies and 35% of sales dollars in service organizations. Quality costs identify opportunities for quality improvement and establish funding priorities by means of Pareto analysis. This analysis allows the quality improvement program to concentrate on the vital quality problem areas. Once corrective action has been completed, the quality costs will measure the effectiveness of that action in terms of dollars. Optimization is very important. Failure costs are optimized when there are no identifiable and profitable projects for reducing them. Appraisal costs are also optimized when there are no identifiable and profitable projects for reducing them. To understand benchmarks in performance the current process has to be documented and understood. Several techniques such as flow diagrams and cause and effect diagrams should be understood. Careful questioning is necessary and process resources have to be understood. Benchmarking studies can reveal three different outcomes, like a negative gap, where the external processes may be significantly better than the internal processes. Parity, where process performance is approximately equal or positive gap where internal process is found to be superior to external processes. There are two ways to prove that one practice is superior to another. If processes compared are clearly understood and adequate performance measures are available, the practices can be analyzed quantitatively. Summary measures and ratios, such as activity costs, return on assets, defect rates, or customer satisfaction levels can be calculated and compared.

In the quality management system the organization shall establish, document, implement, and maintain a QMS and continually improve its effectiveness. The organization shall identify needed processes such as management activities, provision of resources, product realization, and measurement. It determines the sequence and interaction, determines criteria and methods for effective operation and control of these processes and ensure the availability of resources and information necessary to support and monitor these processes. It monitors, measures and analyzes these processes and implement actions to achieve planned result and continuous improvement of these processes. Outsourced processes that affect the quality of the product is identified and included in the system. Design and development outputs shall meet the input requirements for design and development and look towards purchasing, production and service provision, shall meet the product acceptance criteria and specify the characteristics of the product for its safe and proper use. Measuring equipment shall be calibrated and verified at frequent intervals, and it can be measured or recorded and the equipment can be readjusted with use.

Instead of working on what the customer expects, work is concentrated on fixing what the customers does not want. By implementing QFD an organization is guaranteed to implement the voice of the customer in the final product or service. Quality function deployment helps identify new quality technology and job functions to carry out operations. This tool provides a historic reference to enhance future technology and prevent design errors. QFD is primarily a set of graphically oriented planning matrices that are used as the basis for decisions affecting any phase of the product development cycle. Results of QFD are measured based on the number of design and engineering changes, time to market, cost and quality. It is considered by many experts to be a perfect blueprint for quality by design. Quality function deployment enables the design phase to concentrate on the customer requirements, thereby spending less time on redesign and modifications. The saved time has been estimated at one-third to one-half of the time taken for redesign and modification using traditional means. The saving means reduced development cost and also additional income because the product enters the market sooner. When an organization decides to implement QFD, the project managers and team members need to be able to commit a significant amount of time to it, especially in the early stages. There are two types of teams-designing a new product or improving an existing product. The existing product team usually has fewer members, because the QFD process will only need to be modified. Time and inter-team communication are two very important things that each team must utilize to their fullest potential. Team meetings are very important in the QFD processes. The team leader needs to ensure that the meetings are run in the most efficient manner and that the members are kept informed. The meeting format should have some way of measuring how well the QFD process is working at each meeting and should be flexible, depending on certain situations. The duration of the meetings will rely on where the teams members are coming from and what needs to be accomplished. Shorter meetings allow information to be collected between times that will ensure that the right information is being entered in the QFD matrix. QFD takes the experience and information that are available within an organization and puts them together as a structured format that is easy to assimilate. Fewer engineering changes are required when using QFD, and when used properly, all conflicting design requirements can be identified and addressed prior to production. This results in a reduction in retooling, operator training, and changes in traditional quality control measures. By using QFD, critical items are identified and can be monitored from product inception to production. Because QFD concentrates on customer expectations and needs, a considerable amount of effort is put into research to determine customer expectations. This process increases the initial planning stage of the project definition phase in the development cycle. The driving force behind QFD is that the customer dictates the attributes of a product. Customer satisfaction, like quality, is defined as meeting or exceeding customer expectations. Sources for determining customer expectations are focus groups, surveys, complaints, consultants, standards and federal regulations. It is the job of the QFD team to analyze these customer expectations into more specific customer requirements. The goal of the QFD is not only to meet as many customer expectations and needs as possible, but also to exceed customer expectations. Each QFD team must make its product either more appealing than the existing product or more appealing than the product of a competitor. The QFD team or preferably the focus group ranks each customer requirement by assigning it a rating. Assigning ratings to customer requirement is sometimes difficult, because each member of the QFD team might believe that different requirements should be ranked higher. The importance rating is useful by prioritizing efforts and making trade-off decisions. By looking towards the design techniques and by using quality by design, the product is designed within production capabilities in order for statistical process control to be effective. Producing products well within process capabilities will cause a chain reaction of customer satisfaction. Customer returns will decrease and rework costs will also decrease. Profit margin becomes larger, because the time that was used to rework in-house non-conformities and customer returns can now be used to produce new products. Quality by design provides manufacturers with the tools and communication and management techniques required to develop products in a timely and cost-effective manner from the beginning and throughout the products life. Quality by design utilizes prior experience, emphasize early high quality designs, support the fulfillment of customer requirements, feedback constraints and look at conceptual design and sales. In its organizational structure, information paths are opened up between departments in different disciplines. A field service employee can talk directly with a production engineer about a common service problem that could be easily remedied in the production phase of product development. This facility helps in opening of communication paths between employees and their subsequent empowerment in decision making process. Design for manufacture and assembly (DFMA) is a design philosophy that identifies production and assembly problems. Software programs alert engineers of design problems prior to production. Potential problems, such as excessive costs due to part complexity, number of parts, difficult assembly procedures, increased assembly times, and unreasonable or unwarranted tolerances, and changes in a design can be made before design effort continues, or before full production commences. DFMA has evolved to also include design for service and design for environment. In design for service, a product or process is designed, for efficient repair and maintenance by establishing assembly and disassembly sequences, generating a degree of difficulty and time estimate for service and identifying the service life of particular parts. In design for environment, a product or process is designed such that its disposal presents to adverse environmental impact while being cost-effective.

Designing an FMEA or failure mode and effect analysis aids in the design process by identifying known and foreseeable failure modes and then ranking failures according to relative impact on the product. Implementing design FMEA helps establish priorities based on expected failures and severity of those failures and helps uncover oversights, misjudgments, and errors that may have been made. Design FMEA reduces development time and cost of manufacturing processes by eliminating many potential failure modes prior to operation of the process and by specifying the appropriate test to prove the designed product. Process FMEA is used to identify potential process failure modes by ranking failures and helping to establish priorities according to the relative impact on the internal or external customer. Implementing process FMEA helps to identify potential manufacturing or assembly causes in order to establish controls for occurrence reduction and detection. The FMEA evaluation should be conducted immediately following the design phase of product production and in most cases, before purchasing and setting up any machinery. FMEA compares design characteristics relative to the planned manufacturing or assembly modes so that the product meets customer requirements. A process FMEA is required for all new parts/processes, changed parts/processes and carryover parts/processes in new applications or environments. It is initiated before the feasibility stage, prior to tooling for production, and take into account all manufacturing operations, from individual components to assemblies.

The total productive maintenance function should be directed towards the elimination of unplanned equipment and planned maintenance. The objective is to create a system in which all maintenance activities can be planned and not interfere with the production process. Surprise equipment breakdowns should not occur. TPM is merely trying to tap into an unused resource, the brain power and problem-solving ability of all the organizations employees. Thus it allows people to make decisions. After this step we come to the process known as experimental design. Any experiment that has flexibility to make desired changes in the input variables of a process to observe the output response is known as experimental design. It is a systematic manipulation of a set of variables in which the effect of these manipulations is determined, conclusions are made and results are implemented. A good experiment must be efficient. It is not an isolated test but a well planned investigation that points the way toward understanding the process. Knowledge of the process is essential to obtain the required information and achieve the objective. Statistical process control (SPC) methods and experimental design technique are powerful tools for the improvement and optimization of a process, system, design and so forth. SPC assumes that the right variable is being controlled, the right target is known and that the tolerance is correct. Experimental design is known as active statistical method. Information is extracted for process improvement based on tests done on the process, changes made in the input and observations of the output. Similarly tolerance design is the process of designing the statistical tolerance around the target. During the parameter design stage, low cost tolerancing should be used. Only when the values are beyond the low cost tolerancing limits is this concept implemented. Tolerance design is the selective tightening of tolerances or upgrading to eliminate excessive variation. Thus this chapter includes the most important sub-parts of TQM and thus describes how the modern world quality control techniques have changed.

Chapter 9

Total quality control and plant performance
(BY BAISHAM CHATTERJEE)

Most people in industry readily recognize products and services as the output of industrial effort and quality control is that type of output. Project works and management systems is another type of output. Projects are the project industry counterpart of products in the manufacturing industry; management systems are the counterpart of services. Division into product producing companies or service providing companies is not always easy, because all companies use mix of both. If a company takes a range of products and uses a range of services, and from them brings into being a complex work, such as airport, harbor, high-rise building, or retirement village then it falls in the project industry group. If the quality of output from an industry like MIL-Q-9858 is applied to the training of soldiers, the operating of a chain of beauty shops or a whole range of services providing activities. Although there are controls in the manufacturing industry that are applicable, other controls in the manufacturing standard are so different and so lacking that it cannot make an adequate degree of quality control in services or project industry.

Application of MIL-Q-9858, or its derivative standards, to services providing or to project type work, many of the requirements of control areas in the two kinds of industry have not been met. Further endeavor of quality standards and general procedures reveals that there are only three kinds: mass manufacturing, services, and the project (construction) industries. Quality standards for the mass-manufacturing industry have been found unsuitable by professional quality engineers working in the services and project industries. Thus individual segments of the latter two kinds of industries have had to undertake self-regulation and prepare regulatory standards for themselves, as in the case of nuclear power industry with the assistance of the jurisdictional authority concerned.

Similarly design and development work will ordinarily be in-house designs or it is done under contract for a customer. When contract requirements differ from similar requirements of this procedure, the contract requirements will override the stated or implied requirements of this procedure. It is possible in great majority of these industries, and they will be found applicable in most design situations and contracts. All design and development work involves a succession of compromises between alternatives, and often conflicting requirements and capabilities. Design of more complex products with more demanding operational requirements will require more sophisticated design organizations with varied backup and support facilities. The customer way, through design reviews monitor the progress of the design. They develop trials and tests to be carried out. If so the stage is complete only when they have been done and the results have been analyzed. As in the case of final design model, it would be possible to estimate the costs of production, including test and production equipment and staff involved. During the strategic stages of the design work it is important to carry out in-house formal design reviews, ongoing awareness and quantitative knowledge of progress and success or failure of the design can be acquired. In all new designs there is often new and a certain amount of highly original work representing first time creation. In routine applications there is often good design practices and existing design standards. During an assessment of a suppliers design and development capabilities, the assessors converse with suppliers managers and staff, read company documents, observe the design work that is going on and examine design support facilities and design tools. In a project type work the need for changes in the operational requirements of the finished product will sometimes arise. The need may arise at any time during the design and development phase on the part of the supplier. The customer or marketing department shall approve it for in-house use. When the design contract calls for product development as the final contract phase and the item developed is the item to be delivered, along with the design, each necessary control and activity required for bringing the product into being shall be a subject of the part of the planning review. Design work is not solely conceptual and laboratory oriented, supported by calculations and logic there is need for data generation and documentation as well.

The first type of design work requires a creative insight to the particular need which often goes beyond logic and is capable of producing concepts that reach to the core of the problem. The second type of design work is pragmatic, methodical, and detailed, and it covers all relevant factors and eliminates all uncertainties from the design. Modern computing capabilities with appropriate graphic capabilities for computer aided design are essential to efficient use of technical skills in design work. Income expansion expenditures in the area of design and development are a most profitable form of expenditure for companies, and the ownership of original and creative work results is a matter for contractual agreement prior to beginning the work. Test specifications and reports of any test results and detailed records of the design, including software programs, specifications, drawings, parts list and control drawings. Value engineering is an organized program by which operational requirements can be met while providing the lowest life cycle cost. The value of quality can be adjusted to be met at the lowest compatible cost of quality.

Looking at the organization perspective the contractor shall delegate to the personnel managing and carrying out software design and development activities clear responsibility and authority for the control of quality in all work carried out under the contract. Operational requirements specification and its supporting documentation detailing function, environment and language are needed to carry out the design, coding, and formal qualification and testing using flowcharts and detailed program requirements. Operator caused variability, machine caused variability, machine setup caused variability and management caused variability in the products manufacturing industry, and no 3 and 4 in this become predominant and with high operator input and 1 and 4 are major causes of variability. The products manufacturing industry has mastered the production of high quality equipment to such a degree that the equipment seldom contributes to poor quality service. The designer shall follow up the identification and documentation of service modules with an in depth design of each module into the total services providing system of the company. Each module shall be measurable by the company in respect to which and to what degree the customer has availed to the particular service module. The service designer shall design into the operations of the company the capability to control, extend, contract, create, or cancel service modules. Communications provided for from the customer to the company shall be designed to provide the company with measures of adequacy, satisfaction, customer well being and other quality characteristics. Variety shall be provided by designing a range of different modules offering different services or the same service in different ways and degrees. Each such module for a given type of service shall possess a routine sameness each time it is accessed so the customer can become confident in the service and rely upon accessing it successfully each time.

It is possible to ascertain the probable differences for an equipment by considering any differences in system assembly, parts count and parts reliability. When the system assembly configuration in an equipment has inherently higher reliability, then it can be predicted to have higher reliability than the first one. For equipments undergoing normal technological evolution and especially improved models from one company it is possible to arrive at good qualitative estimates of the relative reliabilities of the later generation systems from the known performance of the earlier generation systems. Outputs from design reviews, parts-derating policies, joining and assembly training, part selection and application procedures, part-screening programs, failure analysis to determine failure modes, criticality analysis, and maintenance programs are collected and analyzed to determine the contributions of each area to the overall system unreliability. The differences between people in understanding concepts go further than just parts, subsystems and systems as seen by one person. What one company considers to be the system it is designing and producing a customer of that company will fit with a number of equally complex systems into an operating system that is even more complex overall. Examination of the system from an analytical viewpoint is called a top-down view. In this stage the designer selects the configuration for the system, selects the subsystems and reaches decisions on how they will be joined, and selects the parts and raw materials of which the subsystems will be constructed. Each of these activities and decisions contributes to or detracts from the ultimate system reliability. Synthesizing the system begin at the raw material and component level. Choice of raw materials to meet a specific reliability goal is of major importance in system design. Starting at the bottom and building the system from its many materials and parts results in an examination of each material and part, from the standpoint of its reliability and function. This approach also causes the designer to give due consideration to the many methods of joining and packaging the various materials and parts together into the subsystems and ultimately the system.

Shock and vibration, or motion-type considerations, have major influences on equipment reliability. These aspects shall be treated in depth adequate to ensure that the equipment will have the ability to perform in accordance with the operational performance specifications. Chemical reactions, often over extended periods of time, will determine whether many types of equipment will have the reliability required. These included chemical actions as corrosion, chemical change of liquids like lubricants and deterioration of adhesive materials. The design limits, unless rationalized with production after production starts will be exceeded and the reliability ratings on the equipment may be no longer valid. A source of unreliability is to be found in the production materials, techniques, and production equipment as well as test facilities which were not encountered during design and development. Two factors that arise from this situation must be covered. The first is the need to ensure, each time a deviation occurs, the degree of deviation and its inference for the reliability of the equipment must be known and acceptable. The second with the cooperation of designers and manufacturing engineers brings a complete design production drawing rationalization after the start-up of production. Another source of unreliability is found in the maintenance activity established to keep the equipment operating. The advancing technological nature of products will cause increasingly rapid obsolescence.

In order to source quality control the company shall provide for and carry out sufficient quality checks or surveillance at a suppliers facilities to ensure that the quality of supplies is achieved and maintained. The decision to carry out source checks or surveillance shall be based on the benefits that will derive from each situation. The contribution to the finished product quality and the cost effectiveness of the activity shall be based on the benefits and factors that are used to make the decision. In case of suppliers the company shall provide for control of the quality of all material received from suppliers. When it is appropriate to the overall quality plan, such incoming material shall be subject to quality characteristics. It is important to provide adequate methods for identifying purchased material. It can also identify test status of the material as needed for traceability. Source inspected items validate documentation of inspections and testing performed on the items and the condition of items after shipment. Help in storage, handling, protection and controlled release of purchased material. Bringing together a bit different outlook, it is special processes that have parameters that affect product characteristics but cannot be economically controlled or economically measured by in-process inspection or test that assure the stability of the processing and measuring equipment involved in the processes by periodically verifying the accuracy and variability of the equipment.

The company's quality control program shall extend to encompass the sales, delivery, installation, and use of its products. Products shall be designed for specific purposes and design specifications shall contain user or consumer requirements information against which the products shall be assessed. The company shall establish direct and indirect contacts with its customers for the purpose of communicating and collecting data and other information needed to develop its specifications and provide total satisfaction. Corrective action creates a change in some element of the manufacturing activity. Any such change shall be permitted to occur only in an orderly and controlled way. The quality system shall provide for recording and classifying all instances of unsatisfactory quality, with particular attention being given to repetitive occurrences. They shall be correlated according to such common factors as product type, failure mode and material supplier. Product failures shall be ranked according to cost, and corrective action shall be taken accordingly. The choice of a control method is usually left up to the person in charge of work to be done. In project work the control of the project must be strongly administered from the individual or organization designated as the project manager. In capital works and building construction that is the prime contractor; in manufacturing industry, control emanates from senior manager to whom designer, developer, producer and quality assurance people report, with the designer providing technical guidance throughout. There should be control on the ongoing processing, fabrication, delivery, installation or commissioning of items containing nonconformities through to the stage at which verification establishes the satisfactory disposition of the earlier questioned items. In the quality control process it is important to identify each point in the manufacturing and construction cycle at which inspections, tests, process controls, tryouts, or other verifications are to be employed. These shall cover vendor items, incoming items, preservation of items, packaging, site inspection and all commissioning activities.

A principal aspect of the quality control plan shall be the designed configuration of the finished work or product constructed under the contract. The company would prepare plans for the periodic review of work underway to ascertain that the configuration of the end work or product is being maintained. These plans shall call for configuration assessment and review following any change in design and any change in materials, processes, methods of joining, or other change which may affect the configuration of the end work or product. Assessment and measurement of the products or services shall be competent in their work and have knowledge and skills adequate to successfully and objectively make measurements and assessments necessary to verify that the products or services meet specified requirements. The company shall decide to prepare, implement and maintain a program for the systematic review and audit of the quality system established in accordance with this procedure. The audit shall ensure the continuing suitability and effectiveness of the quality system. The company shall establish and maintain an effective quality system for inspections and tests on products or services in their completed stages. This shall include documented procedures for final inspection and test operations, including workmanship standards and quality records. Design changes to items shall always be tested in working models of the items throughout all relevant item operational requirements before they are considered satisfactory. The results obtained from such tests shall be documented and made a part of the item design history file for later review when required. Control of changes made during the design phase of an item shall be by the design manager who has control of the overall design project. When it is appropriate, design changes shall receive the approval of the customer or any jurisdictional authority. Tests consistently verify that materials and sub-assemblies are fully conforming. Completed item testing shall show that outgoing items consistently and fully conform to operational requirements. In such an operation it is possible to operate at the highest profit level. Change shall therefore be naturally resisted and considered an undesirable aspect of mass production.

The calibration control system procedure defines the requirements of the company for control systems. It defines the requirements for a system to be established and used in ensuring the measuring equipment, standards, and certified reference materials (CRMs) are properly calibrated or certified and that the company's measuring equipment and CRMs are satisfactory for use in verifying the conformance to contract of materials designed, developed, produced, or repaired and services offered. The company shall conduct, during the earliest phase of contract or purchase order performance, an extensive review of technical requirements of the contract and set standards necessary for the successful discharge of work. Calibration procedures shall include such documents as manufacturers manuals, published standard practices, and any necessary written instructions of the company or the producer of the measurement instruments, including step-by-step calibration sequences documented for use by calibration personnel. All CRMs used to determine values for materials used in products and to determine processes that control product characteristics shall have their sources in or be traceable to the national standards laboratory or other organization responsible for providing such materials in the nation. When a calibration equipment is transferred to a different place, consideration shall be taken for changes in temperature, humidity, cleanliness or other environmental factors.

After the last step the conduct of the quality audit is carried out by examining the people, tools, premises, surroundings, and manufacturing or providing processes which collectively comprise the quality system. The examination is carried out against specific standards and procedures which should always be nominated prior to start of the audit. The audit examines the control trail all the way from what went into the wording of the procurement contract or purchase order specifying levels of control of the quality characteristics of supplies, as well as the limits like production, testing, handling, packing, delivery, unpacking, labeling, sampling, inspection and testing, procedures for passing satisfactory material and delivering it to stock and preservation of quality characteristics during such activities. The audit shall examine the use of instruments for any lack of calibration currency, the instrument recall system for preventive maintenance and calibration methods and effectiveness, the calibration frequency practice in use, the method of initial setting of calibration frequency, in accordance with calibration standard. The calibration audit examines the conditions of use and the environments of these instruments and its handling and storage and its bearing on instrument accuracy. Identify hazard, degree and scope that helps to recall coordinator convenes product recall committee. It is important to transfer to recall coordinator to control and follow. These are all the product recall, repair or replace actions. Halt production of offending items; notify of hazard and its nature; enter all known data to date on problem; and maintain log. Product recall committee reviews and approves media communications; customers and distributors. Determine locations of all known hazardous products; send notices to each; stop distribution and sales. In order to recall product, determine storage and calculate disposal of returns it is important to place recall orders, with replacement instructions, to relevant recipients; and arrange transport, receipt, storage and disposal of returns.

Manufacturing industry has as its goal the design and production of products which will have the design characteristics and production quality needed to satisfy customers throughout the lifetime of the products. Products have those attributes within an overall economic system that suits the customers ideas of quality for reasonable price and acceptable profit. There is no limit to the size of the production activity which can benefit from the use of quality cost control in addition to processing cost control, nor is there a limit to the type of production activity which will benefit. All companies who process raw materials into finished goods, assemble parts into finished systems, or through project activity, assemble parts into operational utilities of major proportions will be able to use the principles of quality cost control to their profitable advantage. It will be necessary for the quality manager and accounting manager to work closely in separating processing and quality costs, recording each, and analyzing and reporting these costs of doing business. It is the quality managers duty to coordinate the adjustment of quality costs by other organizations so that optimum cost distribution and minimum total cost of operation are achieved in respect to quality activities. Cost reporting on a basis of direct labor dollar expenditure will be changed when new automated machinery is installed in the plant and the number of process operators in the area changes. Depreciation costs of plant and buildings are readily understood accounting cost cells. Similarly, interest cost on money borrowed, invested and used for manufacturing are normal areas of expenditure and accounting. Opportunity budgets reflect the nearness of any new product production or major improvements and the magnitude of efforts by the relevant cost centre for their activities. Larger opportunity budgets are carried by product activities, marketing, design and sales. Then as the production schedule is planned the opportunity budget will decrease and operating budget will increase to handle the new effort. Cost control reports from the accounting organization have traditionally contained only process costs, within which have been buried a portion of the quality costs, intermixed and understood. It may be visible to the subject of manipulation, adjustment, and control in order to ensure that a desired outcome will eventuate. The analysis of quality costs is an essential part of the capability and quality costs by themselves are not adequate for conveying their individual degrees of significance. A sum of money on its own, without someone's ability to view it relative to some chosen base of overall monetary control, does not convey its importance. It is necessary to be able to see the individual quality costs in terms of the various cost standards chosen for the business. These cost standards are chosen measures of business performance such as standard sales dollar, standard dollar of direct production labor, and standard dollar of processing cost. It is usually the total quality cost, or quality cost in areas like prevention, appraisal or failure which is compared to the reference base to give a suitable significance. The business problem in the market resolves itself into two considerations: the manufacturing company's economics vs the customers total cost related to the product. In the consumer market, the usual result is the optimization of the manufacturers cost and the corresponding development of a service and replacement industry. It is necessary to optimize both the manufacturers cost and the customers total cost by careful design and production of appropriate quality products.

Determination of the points of control and the amount of inspection and testing required shall be integrated with the planning of the processing, with feedback loops being shortened to the optimum degree and the cost of making each measurement being analyzed and reduced to a minimum consistent with the needs of the product. After the flowcharts covering processing, inspection and testing is prepared. The relationship between prevention and failure is so sensitive that, in a plant experiencing high failure rates, only a small expenditure in key prevention areas will be required to get a major drop in failure rates. When control of required quality characteristics in materials and components is inadequate, there develops a need to apply greater expenditures in appraising, screening, and sorting produced items in order to obtain items acceptable for shipment. This is accompanied by a high level of scrap and rework activity going on in parallel. Nonconformance in raw materials and components will reduce the need for great amounts of appraisal consequent to the lack of such preventive effort. Two factors influence the degree of optimization to be sought in this area. One is the economics of the overall production operation; the other is the matter of safety and liability incurred by the company in this respect. In the absence of the safety problem, the management aim shall be to achieve a balance between expenditure on prevention of faults and nonconformance throughout the total activity and expenses incurred through product failure.

After completing the systems control aspect, to think of things in a different aspect. The first job of quality control may be termed new design control. Included here is the quality control effort on a new product while its marketable characteristics are being selected; while design parameters are being established and proved by prototype tests; while the manufacturing process is being planned and initially costed; while the quality standards are specified. Both product and process designs are reviewed to eliminate possible sources of quality troubles before the start of formal production to improve maintainability and to eliminate threats of product reliability. In quantity production, new design control ends when pilot runs have given proof of satisfactory production performance, and with job shop production the routine ends as work is being started on production of the component parts. The second job of quality control is incoming material control. Involved here are the procedures for actual acceptance of materials, parts, and components purchased from other companies from other operating units. A number of quality control techniques are applied to provide acceptance at most economical levels. The techniques include vendor quality evaluations; certification of materials, parts, and components by the vendor; acceptance sampling techniques and laboratory tests. It is important to determine quality procedures for controlling product and process quality, including reliability requirements.

Looking at the cost-wise factor of total quality control, at first when prevention costs are increased to pay for the right kind of engineering work in quality control, a reduction in the number of product defects occurs. This defect reduction means a substantial reduction in failure costs. Second, the same chain of events takes place with appraisal costs. An increase in prevention costs results in defect reduction, which in turn have a positive effect on appraisal costs, since defect reduction means a reduced need for routine inspection and test activities. Finally when there is upgrading of quality control equipment, personnel and practices an additional reduction in appraisal cost results. Better inspection and test equipment, a general modernization of quality control practices, and the replacement of many routine operators by less numerous but more effective process control inspectors and tests have a positive downward pull on the cost of the appraisal function.

Behind the idea of developing a quality system plan, production evaluation in the case of a preproduction quality evaluation should be done, where feasible, under actual end-use conditions. Environments should be duplicated, even to the extent of matching the skills of the persons expected to understand and operate the device. Such an operator should be given the instructions that will be supplied. During the preproduction quality evaluation, other important tasks that are accomplished are finding out the quality characteristics; review of specifications for clarity, compatibility and economy; location and elimination of sources of manufacturing troubles and out of control quality problems before start of manufacture; identification of adjustments to design or process to make them compatible. In the quality information feedback specific procedures are established which implement data collection, tabulation, analysis and distribution. Formats for the following kinds of reports should be developed: incoming-material quality evaluations, end of line quality evaluations, product reliability and life evaluations, manufacturing losses, in process quality audits, field failure and service call rates, special studies reports, quality costs and quality system measurement reports. Periodic review of the quality information system is necessary to keep it current in meeting the changing needs of the company.

The quality information equipment subsystem provides the procedures for procuring this measurement and control equipment. Such activity has advanced development aspects which include study of the long-range needs of the company's business with respect to measuring equipment on the basis of new products, new processes, and improvements in product quality, flow, and costs. During prototype testing, it is necessary carefully to log the history of the prototype as to the characteristics of materials along with any special operations or processes required to produce it. Quality planning is performed through this. When a design engineer starts the product design, there are certain functional objectives he is trying to meet with the product. What is considered is what is possible from a design standpoint within the limitations of delivery time and prices but also what is possible from a manufacturing point. Dimensional characteristics are as a matter of fact, but one of a long list of quality characteristics needed for the evaluation of today's products. A whole array of electronic parameters must be measured: voltage, current, power, resistance, capacitance, and frequency in a wide range of values. Chemical measurements are becoming increasingly common, even in the mechanical goods and electrical industries. Physical strength, thrust, flow, pressures, temperatures, and times (in microseconds) are more and more widely used measurements. There are many advanced development programs. Whether applicable to existing or to new products, the advanced development program are dependent upon, and to a large extent guided by, the advanced planning being carried on in the quality control engineering area. When new product designs are involved, the quality information equipment design cycle must also integrate with the work of the product planning group which is materializing new product specifications; it must also continue into the detailed design of the product by engineering. In product planning it is important to review product specifications, make product tolerance studies based on capability analysis, make provision for automatic inspection and tests and provide broad equipment requirements. In the case of design, procurement and construction sketches, layouts, circuit diagrams, itemized material lists and detailed equipment specification sheets are originated. The associated test and inspection operation instructions, developed by quality control engineering technology, are finalized and the required equipment operating instructions and calibration and maintenance procedures are drafted.

In theory, the frequency of making the sample checks may be calculated mathematically. This decision is an economic judgment based on such factors as the numbers of inspectors available, the quality history of the job, the quantity of hourly production and how much it might cost to allow an out of control condition to exist undetected. Instead of computing and plotting the average or medial values for a sample, it can be supposed that the individual limits for each unit in the sample are plotted on the control chart for averages. Suppose that these units are drawn from a sample whose average value is perilously close to the control limit. With control gaging, it is these individual pieces that are examined, it is quite possible and practical to establish gage limits at the control limits for average values and to allow the number of pieces which do not meet these gage limits to stand as an indication as a state of control of the process. It may be necessary to put fully as much rehandling time on a product with an inexpensive defect as is required for a product with an expensive defect. Again the repair cost of these expensive and inexpensive defects tends to balance off in the long run, permitting the consideration that all defects comprising the per cent defective results may be treated of equal weight. They are of 3 types critical defects, major defects and minor defects. There are perfectly reasonable parts of developing control chart installations for a factory, even though they may result in a departure from standard control chart technique. Experience seems to show that in the long run, proponents of the control chart approach in a factory would be most successful if they concentrate upon promoting the fundamental concepts and points of view fostered by the control chart rather than upon endeavoring to push forward any particular control chart technique or form.

A number of independent checks on the reliability of 100 percent inspection in sorting out all bad parts from the good have cast considerable doubt upon its complete effectiveness in every instance. Where the percent defective in lots submitted is low, the monotony of repetitive inspection operations may result in the automatic acceptance of a number of defective parts. In contrast to the liabilities of 100 percent inspection, sampling procedures may be inexpensive. Cost considerations may make it expedient to allow a predetermined percentage of defective parts until that assembly point is reached where they may be removed by production operators who find a difficult assembly. Many well conceived acceptance sampling procedures, such as MIL-STD-105A, also provide for reduced sampling and tightened sampling plans for use of supplant normal sampling under certain circumstances where it is still desired to hit the quality target specified. While these reduced sampling plans do not conform to the OC curves for the normal sampling table in question, their use is justified in that they take advantage of the additional information about the quality of lots submitted that has been obtained from the use of normal sampling schedules. It is most certainly an uneconomical duplication of effort, successively to use both process control and acceptance sampling plans on parts from the same production area. When a carburetor choke on an automobile becomes automatic, there were no simple way to override. When the automatic choke is multiplied by a multitude of the modern more complex products of today-household automatic washers, automatic machine tools, electronic control equipments, automatic electric ranges-the impact of the increased significance of product reliability becomes apparent.

Both product strength and environmental stress values can be affected, sometimes drastically by what happens during manufacture. Much of it is caused by variability in manufacturing process because of variability in the strength of materials due to non-homogeneity, variations in dimensions and variations in composition. When redundancy takes places it reduces the total reliability of the system. In airborne equipment, redundancy increases weight; which is to be avoided. It increases initial costs and maintenance costs and redundancy should never be introduced in designs. There may for example, be no organized means for feeding back to the design engineer information from the plant laboratory about new materials or processes. Mechanical inspection or electrical testing groups may be forced to wait for information on what they should inspect or test until production have started and many defective units have been scrapped. Parts tolerances may be selected with no knowledge of or reference to the accuracies that may be actually held on the plants machine tools and processes. Sales efforts in product planning and merchandising may work in directions opposed to the design actually being developed. Desirable cost standards for parts inspection sampling or bogeys for manufacturing losses may be established only after the design has been in active production for a considerable length of time.

By sketching specification limits on the frequency distribution pictures, the engineer secures at a glance an indication as to whether the 4ZP96B3 as designed will perform within specification limits and whether the company can expect a minimum of rejects if specifications are followed throughout. Where the required product improvements are difficult to make or where the expenditures necessary to eliminate the difficulties would be very high, the decision as to whether to live with the rejects resolves into a problem of economics that must be solved by plant top management. The conclusion of the new design control activities is the formal release, after a final review design of the 4ZP96B3 for active production.

Inadequate utilization may be made of modern statistical acceptance sampling tables. Incoming materials may be damaged by poor handling during its receipt and travel through the plant. Certain materials which are placed on the shelf after incoming acceptance-like insulating strips may be harmed due to improper storage facilities. Ineffective means for tagging and disposing materials found defective may result in occasional lots of the material finding their way into active production. These instances illustrate the first of the two aspects in which the incoming material procedures of many factories have been unsatisfactory in assisting plant management to achieve its quality-product goal: these incoming material procedures have too often permitted defective materials to be accepted by the plant for use in its production line. The second aspect in which these incoming control procedures have been inadequate is more directly related to economics. In some plants, incoming material routines have been unnecessarily cumbersome and drawn out. Too much time and money have been spent to achieve the amount of control that is required for the materials and parts received. Incoming material control involves techniques in purchasing, process control engineering, laboratory and materials handling as well as in other functional fields. It concerns relations with vendors as far as quality is concerned. It applies to all parts and materials received by the factory for use in production; in some plants in introduces control over materials used in plant service and plant protection.

After looking at the issue of total quality control, the availability as a core subsystem for plant and business performance can be taken into account. Here at first the product composition, fitness for use and producibility is judged. The facility to perform its production process is found out and support activities is judged and at last the sales and distribution of the productive capacity created by previous three subsystems is found out. The four subsystems almost completely determine the owners competitiveness, income, and productivity of working and capital assets. Therefore how well the four subsystems are integrated by design and then dynamically managed is critical because short and longer term change are basic realities of the product, production process and sales and distribution subsystems. If any of these money making sub-systems are not appropriately designed and managed, the plant as a production system and the owners business results will suffer. Availability performance is of few important types: availability as a probability distribution function, reliability as the interface characteristic between the product and process subsystem, top level factors of reliability and maintainability. There are a few strategic implications: It is critical to know the location and shape of the achievable availability curve. Otherwise it is not possible to determine what is reasonable and possible for operational availability and therefore plant production. If the upper curve is not known, manufacturing operations management may unknowingly attempt to achieve performance beyond what is possible. Management must make strategic decisions for the long term relative positions of the two curves. As plant production is increased over time, changing operating conditions will drive the upper curve down. Meanwhile, maintenance operation management must progressively move the lower curve upwards to move the demands of production. Additional availability can then be acquired only by a change in plant design. Reliability and maintenance are economically interchangeable in the creation of income. As a choice is skewed towards one characteristic, the life-cycle cost of the specified availability is eventually increased. Failure to capitalize on the interchangeability of the previously introduced reliability and maintainability factors may lead to excessive life-cycle cost. The individual factors behind both are maximized rather than correlated. Plant availability, and therefore the resulting normal cost of overall productive capacity will grossly exceed what is required and plant income will be reduced. In order to become a low cost producer the following points are made: each step of the curve represents a plant and its respective cost structure in terms of product unit cost. Each business cycle has an associated demand, as business conditions worsen. The umbrella product unit price in each business cycle is generally set by market forces to reflect the high-cost producer.

Plant design meets, but does not exceed specified availability. This means that management is not unconsciously investing in productive capacity it did not strategically intend to create. As a result time to payout is decreased and net present value is increased almost as much as the avoided unjustified capital expenditure. The rate of return is also substantially increased. Income is increased. This is the result of developing the most profit effective maintenance operations as part of the plants availability scheme. Capital expenditures and engineering costs do not appear until commercial production begins. They appear as a lengthy period as a depreciation expense. This is very difficult from the cash flow vision of financial consequences. A perception that the owner is automatically served by the least amount of investment rather than profit effective life cycle availability performance is belied. Capital expenditures and functioning costs are matched to the revenues they ultimately produce. This is meaning of income as compared to cash flow. Without this matching, business performance will be difficult to design and measure.

In the case of availability engineering in the basic design stage it is important to incorporate availability requirements in equipment design and specifications. It is important to develop an infrastructure for change, improvement, and data management with respect to life-cycle availability performance. It is important to analyze the plant design for potential failures and determine appropriate maintenance strategies for each. It is necessary to verify that the plant can perform in accordance with the plant owners specified availability and determine the most profitable scheme for achieving that specified performance. A system might be developed to trace the elements of availability management and their linkages. It is part of the deliverable to develop life-cycle improvement, change and data management functions and systems. A task is developed to evaluate the use of financial models in plant and business management. The failure modes, effects and criticality analysis will ultimately determine organizational solutions for each significant failure. The choices are design, production operations, maintenance functions and quality assurance. Permanent plant changes take place due to incorporating new production equipment technology and to increase the plants productive capacity by eliminating the constraints. Data must be gathered and developed for each plant element mainly statistical data. The design of plant level performance does not depend on such perfection. It requires realistic forecasts of performance for each plant element. They are produced by combining expertise and experience with available data. Performance levels has two extremes: at one point is equipment, subassemblies and components and at the other is plant availability performance. One reason for the distinction is statistical reality. Plant level performance is the synthesis of the reliability, maintainability, and economic forecasts of many elements. The system level prediction gravitates to some central results and confidence limits. Consequently, immense time and cost to initially acquire perfect data is not a prerequisite to successful initial availability design. Existing facilities offer three main sources of data like plant production process control systems that routinely collect massive amounts of data, maintenance operations that produce data associated with the time and resources to repair equipment and predictive maintenance procedures and systems that collect data in the process of monitoring the condition of plant equipment.

Candidate models must be identified and screened in identifying the candidate models and transform them into availability models. The first case is to analyze model use in plant life, secondly it is in identifying stages of model development, which is further sub-divided into 2 parts identify candidate models and determine how candidates serve identified requirements which lead to recommending planning & prepare development plans which is further sub-divided into creating a model for timely plant design and execute plan to develop model. These models range from inexpensive desktop systems to very powerful ones. The powerful models are often available through specialized consultants that have developed their own systems. The choice between them is a function of their comparative abilities. The choice may also reflect the consultants ability and willingness to customize baseline version of the model.

Concept design phase is divided into four types availability centered practices control documents, life cycle improvement, change & data management function and systems which both lead to life cycle of the design concept.

The other two sub-parts are gathering and analyzing availability data and plant logic diagrams which both lead to allocating parameters to diagrams and availability centered FMECA whether the previous one is sub-divided into availability model and financial model and the latter one leads to maintenance logic-tree analysis and both of them they lead to plant layout for maintainability and optimizing availability performance which both lead to detail design phase. Achievable availability as a curve is the result of following factors like: plant hard design which determines the location and shape of the curve and therefore establishes possible achievable availability. The maintenance strategies selected by maintenance logic-tree analysis that determines the plants location on the curve which establishes actual achieved availability. Availability is well below suboptimal. The plants element are not operated close to the wear-out point. An analogy is a car in a grueling and long race where a high percentage do not survive the race. Scheduled maintenance can make it survive the race. Scheduled maintenance is an extremely expensive strategy. Cost curve will rise below the right side of the cost valley.

Product quality helps in meeting product specifications. It improves economic and productivity optimums and targets. Process operation parameters within boundaries that are related to safety and environmental hazards and its operations within the limitations of equipment performance and reliability. Assuring that equipment is operated within boundaries for achieving managements specified availability can be defined by the task of optimizing availability performance. Data accumulation from SCADA can be planned to accumulate identified reliability data. The deliverable would receive input from the task of defining a data system that would continuously connect, access and process data over the plants lifetime.

In order to determine materials of construction and corrosion allowances, in the recent scope, piping, materials and corrosion are a significant concern to some types of production plants. Materials engineering determines and specifies the appropriate materials for all points in the production process. It also specifies their corrosion allowances. Alternate strategies are determined when allowances are unacceptable. These include the use of alloys and injections of inhibitors in the process stream. It is necessary to develop flow-sheets for a scheme to serve the plant with utilities. They identify the components for providing electrical, water, air, steam, inert gases, fuels, refrigerants and heating substances. Undertake load and level studies, that determine the timing and fluctuation of demand for each utility. Determine the requirements for tankage, lines and sizes, instrumentation and controls, equipment specifications, etc. Availability engineering will contribute vital information to the procurement of long lead time items. Analysis will determine how critical these items are to availability performance. The design team will then provide availability parameters to procurement that will have been determined by preliminary availability modeling and data collection and analysis. The most important fields of analysis are: where plant performance and safety are sensitive to the quality of the service task. Analysis on failures that have significant repair requirements that affect the calculation of human, materials and facility resources. Maintenance tasks make complex demands on the organization which require analysis to determine full support requirements. Recall high competence in activities like testing, troubleshooting, removing, repairing, replacing, calibrating and servicing. Maintenance task analysis has important sub-parts to provide a means to both collect, extract, apply, and refine massive data and information. Serving corporate, operating company, plant management functions throughout the facility's producing lifetime goes beyond plant maintenance operations and understand the consequences of plant changes and improvements throughout the availability scheme. The data and analysis system most likely will make many uses and include or integrate components of other maintenance operation system. Examples are equipment information, work package and materials systems.

It is no longer widely possible to design equipment for human factors at this phase in plant design. But it is expected that major shortcomings should not be discovered during the execution of this deliverable. The availability centered control documents details the rules for human factors. Project reviews confirm that these practices are incorporated in equipment design, specification and manufacture. In the grass roots plant, maintenance task analysis and procedures are typically not available for the design of equipment for maintainability due to the timing of information in the typical capital project process. It may still be possible to make design changes, limited to aspects like fasteners, handles, test points etc. The few important points for evaluation of the above factor are: The possibilities for standardization are explored by the parts, tools and maintenance equipment cataloging capability made possible by the content of the maintenance task analysis process. Modularization for electrical, electronic and process control equipment will be concerned with: clearly labeled modules and sockets, ease of making connections, size of the subject equipment, proper inclusion of handles and the ability to check and adjust modules as individual units. The maintenance task analysis deliverable included the development of troubleshooting process. Equipment must be assessed to assure that these test points have been created, are appropriate and are located close to the problem, and are clearly marked. Location is important when external equipment is to be used. Labeling is important for avoiding delays in search of equipment, for preventing items from being missed during routine surveillance and servicing, for preventing repair on the wrong item and for preventing injuries.

The relevance of manufacturer recommendations can be improved if the procurement process provides them with appropriate information. This includes plant and equipment availability goals, criteria, parameters and design checklists applicable to the subject item. Certain important parts of determining material resources comes with designing a scheme for modeling resources, that leads to plan and develop system to model resources which is subdivided into two parts like determining service resource levels, scheme & costs and determining consumable resource levels which both can be synthesized into system of requirements and then lead to conducting fielding analysis. Looking at the resources part, extracting resource items for maintenance task leads to 2 parts determining inventory cost factors and making arbitrary stocking decisions, where the first is subdivided into computing economic order quantity and determining buffer levels which both combine to form determining stocking levels of value and leads to establishing inventory control parameters & elements. In a description of the tasks for modeling and determining support facilities and equipments the first format is the designing scheme to model facilities & equipment which leads to planning & developing system for modeling which further lead to analyzing facility & equipment requirements which has two sub-parts design facility & equipment layout and cost analysis that further breaks into synthesizing and maintenance and leads to the construction and start up phase.

Comprehensive training teaches both generic fundamentals and plant specific information, which covers equipment systems and may also teach chemical or physical principles like heat transfer, fluid flow and chemical properties and reactions. Documentation should be used and students informed why specific types of equipment and materials of construction were selected. Mock up models and electronic models may be built to evaluate plant designs.

Short-term planning is also beneficiary of the availability model, which is used to assess the significance of each current failure. The most relevant modeled measure of on-line performance is inherent availability, which the availability expected between scheduled shutdowns. Expected availability is reduced with each failure and the consequences are not always felt until the plants production is reduced or must cease. On-line inherent availability analysis allows the planner to fully understand the true importance of each new failure however the consequences are not always felt until the plants production is reduced or must cease. The consequence of the planning function can range from the realignment of the maintenance operation scheme to the partial redesign of the plant. Thus long range planning is part of availability management rather than just maintenance operations management. Predicted reliability of plant items is partially the result of minimizing the human error in maintenance. It causes plant availability performance to be distorted by the quality of the repair work. Analyzing and defining maintenance of operations has developed a flowchart where the first part is developing process & linkage diagrams of maintenance operations sub-divided into identifying process to use availability processes and identifying function that contribute to AE&M which lead to identifying and integrating maintenance operations computer systems that further lead to defining the maintenance operations organizations and formulate staff level & cost of maintenance operations that together lead to estimating time of each maintenance operations process. The basic process for applying the concept is simple as follows: identifying and understanding the role of each organizational activity, using the understanding of each activity to identify which of the sub-systems it is part of and see to it that the sub-system is dynamic. Project how that dynamic can undermine overall availability performance generally and other functions specifically. The maintenance field operations should not house the functions that analyze and respond to changing owner needs. Another example is that the same maintenance should not be structured to have inappropriate influence in the determination of support resource levels.

If uncertainty is great, goals and objectives will have to be set and reset throughout some work processes. This requires additional decision making. The structure of upward managers must again be called upon to address new challenges. And as before, the managers will eventually become exhausted by the demands to process information and make associated decisions. In case of reducing performance to an acceptable lower level the availability organization may respond to its challenge by increasing the human, material and other supporting resources. This may be preferable to better managing a lower level of resources while still achieving the same performance. Cross-organization forms can be contrasted with self-containment. Both increase discretion at lower level. The self contained strategy is possible when there is necessary sharing of resources and expertise across outside functions and work processes. Many manufacturing plants are victims of default decisions. This can begin in its design phase if availability engineering is omitted from the project scope. Lowered performance may be because the plant is overdesigned. The same performance would have been possible with hard design and maintenance operations developed in the integrated availability scheme. In the case of determining the structural strategies for the flow of information and decisions it may be possible to accept lower performance in some acceptable form for functions that are classified as minor. The vertical information strategy is made possible by the availability centered data management system. Thus the designers will determine which factors depend on its data and analyses elements. Many functions are served by lateral relations where the goal is to determine which of the organizational methods will be applied to relate the subject functions and work processes. the most detailed construction drawings are as follows: preparing mechanical flow-sheets for review and construction and update equipment list and instrument index. Review and finalize the detailed plant plot and equipment layout and for some plants like chemical production process facility, update the line list and complete detailed piping design. Preparing final utility loads and level determination, utility flow-sheets, and detailed utility system design, drawings and specification. Another important form of plant design is by completing the loss control design with respect to hardware, procedures, protection of materials, and other requirement to protect against or respond to each identified hazard. The design of the plant safety warning and response system and its sub-systems are part of this deliverable. Availability design would also affect the selection of candidate manufacturers, quality assurance and control requirements and processes to review supplier documents. Sensitivity analysis may indicate the need to stress comparative qualifications and experience with respect to assemblies and components within the subject equipment item. It is also possible that the non-traditional designer-supplier relationship programs are made more relevant to plant design, because the manufacturers expertise can be a crucial input to the design and sizing of equipment for reliability and maintainability.

To be aware of any changes allowed in the manufacturing of plant equipment, which may come about as an equipment is manufactured, availability management would be made aware of these changes through the procurement and associated quality assurance processes. To confirm points of installation that will affect an equipment items reliability these can be identified by FMECA in the basic design phase. Such points include foundations, equipment anchors, structures, pipe bracing and in this precision alignment is also a reliability issue where if installed improperly these items create stresses on equipment that will greatly decrease its life and time between failures. The planning for start-up is important to evaluate management policies and decisions for start up. The fundamental responsibilities in start-up include availability engineering, maintenance etc is when the degree and specifics is involved in deliverables and their review during the plant design phase. There are decisions for partial commissioning which are important for their impact on existing operations, safety and hazards control. There are potential risks to safety and productivity from operating some parts of the plant while finishing others. The basic policy for quality assurance and control are far reaching and relevant to the plant's entire life cycle and includes plant design; procurement of equipment for designing specifications; construction and installation and testing of equipment; and plant functioning. The various cost estimates may have been drafted during the concept design phase or if not it can be drafted in the engineering and construction contractors project execution plans. This deliverable will test the assumption of such earlier cost and schedule. From early and evolving project schedules, start up management must determine when the start-up team must be on-site and for how long. However the analysis of the costs and schedule is not limited to the start up team members. It must include the human resource requirements for periodically supporting the team and its functions and should assure that the construction estimates include the necessary crafts. It has to be determined whether plant reliability, maintainability, and availability characteristics and economics have been affected. The review will discover if a design change is needed which are either to reverse the as built condition or counter it which can include the realignment of maintenance operations. Availability maintenance is thus concerned with the earliest possible identification of any divergence from the baseline design where options to change the plant design will become increasingly limited as time passes. As plant and equipment should be subjected to test and evaluation during start-up the maintenance operation functions and elements are also subject to scrutiny as these opportunities arise.

The plant sub-systems may be commissioned individually rather than commissioned for the entire plant. This may be the order of utilities, laboratory, input building handling, ancillary equipment, stages of production and reaction, product storage and materials handling. The objective is to gain confidence in the sub-systems as an operating system and in the operators ability to control the hazards inherent to commissioning a new production system. The short term capacity to test the plant hard design for availability performance is limited. Reliability and maintainability can only be tested as data and information are collected and analyzed over the long term. This is the purpose of the living analysis capability of the availability scheme. Availability performance is only possible in terms of whether maintenance operations, field actions, and resources are appropriately provisioned, effective and efficient as planned. The limitation of limited number of short term possibilities is why the capacity to design and model plant availability is so crucial. Otherwise there is no legitimate means to confidently establish an expectation of performance which would become apparent much later in the plants life.

The aggregate planning cycle has various names. It is defined as the cycle of matching productive capacity with forecasted demand. They incorporate current strategies and resource position. The domain is the owners company-wide aggregate capacity to produce a product. There is always a process with the purpose of matching productive capacity to market demand and other strategic and constraining issues. An example, is an oil and gas exploration and production organization.

Aggregate planning is generally an implicit process within the production departments field development decisions and associated operating budgets. The living availability design is an aggregate planning tool for exploring the ramifications of reducing productive capacity. The objective is to determine how to shift the break-even capacity utilization rate downward. In other words, to shift downward the rate the plant must run be to break even which is done by shifting the current operational availability downward. It is assumed that the vital design activities such as availability engineering were not omitted earlier from the plant capital project and it was very fruitful sometimes for modern and futurist project tasks and management. The long term optimization developed by such processes greatly determine the financial results that can ultimately appear in the operating budget. If the plant is not methodically designed initially to most effectively achieve the specified life cycle availability its operating budgets will reflect the negative financial consequences and are conditions that are less fixed in the short term. Considering the consequences of availability engineering during plant design to the operating budget, the plant is designed from the beginning to be able to most profitably produce managements specified life cycle availability. This was tied to financial, operating and availability performance requirements that were based on complex strategic issues.

Each strategic cycle will have either continued the existing availability scheme or formulated a definitive preliminary design for a new scheme. It is now refined and optimized if it constitutes a change of hard design. Meanwhile, the research and development cycle will have advanced the owners ability to design availability performance. The strategic nature of availability performance must be converted to measurable plant performance at the level of plant sub-systems in order to confirm that specified availability performance will be possible to establish measures for guiding design decisions which begins by studying the plant conceptual design. In order to determine and acquire data development needs, the revised design will require the development of new availability forecasts with respect to reliability, maintainability, and economics. The task of reliability identified points to physical change which is concerned with changed operating conditions. Plant elements will be affected by these changes even though they themselves are not physically changed and reflected in the economics of plant element. The plant subsystems have been distinguished as a normal task in each plant design cycle which must be reevaluated for their response to the current aggregate plan. The plant availability model may be adjusted to depict necessary performance during the aggregate planning horizon. The model shows the elements allocated to the plant subsystem which are developed to define proforma performance over the planning period mainly the elements like reliability, maintainability and economic. The plant logic diagrams can be used as a check off and logic tool to identify very specifically what plant items are affected by new operating conditions and are a result of production assigned to plant. Achievable and operational availability will converge at some time in the future, where greater availability for creating productive capacity can only come from plant redesign. The plant cost structure can be substantially reduced which will bring greater change in profits, where resource levels can be maintained with narrower confidence limits and is a result of making repeatedly better tactical decisions.

Conclusion

A very important example of technology that creates innovation and new production strategies is Crown Equipments strategy of designing radically new lift trucks was reinforced by its ability to design and manufacture its own components. Its competitor were constrained from being too innovative because they relied on outside supplier to provide most of its components often based on standard designs incorporated in their products. Crowns ability to customize its products to meet the specific needs of individual customers was due to the fact that it had adopted and perfected a production process whereby batches of various size were assembled to perform a sequence of tasks in the same workplace. New operating abilities often arise in ways and from sources that are difficult to predict. Putting too much reliance on competitive benchmarking, or on monitoring the innovations of ones direct competitors can easily misdirect a company's attention away from the new operating capabilities that are developing in apparently unrelated arenas. Previously unconnected capabilities can be cultivated and combined in a unique way. When capabilities are combined and focused on a new market segment or competitive approach, those being attacked often find it difficult to respond.

An operations capacity often is difficult even to define, much less measure with any accuracy, since it represents a complex interaction of physical space, equipment, operating rates, human resources, system capabilities, company policies and the rate and dependability of suppliers. Capacity cushions should reflect outside processing capacity, like relative cost of having more capacity than needed, the cost of unused plant and equipment and underutilized human resources which can be compared by also developing cost of overtime, subcontracting, and lost profits. The basic trade-off that must be made involve, first, the reduction in the cost per unit that comes from adding a larger chunk of capacity; second, the cost of operating an underutilized facility until demand grows to the point when this additional capacity is needed. A firm can land up with more cost-effective facility and reduced shortage costs. The two other factors are: firstly during periods of sustained economic growth many companies run out of capacity and place orders for new equipment at about the same time, causing equipment costs to rise rapidly. Secondly in many industries technological advancements have occurred with shocking suddenness. This is true to industries that depend heavily on computer or information technology, no industry is immune to such disruption.

If part designs and specifications can be codified precisely and conveyed in standard ways, co-ordination between R&D and manufacturing can be achieved through the exchange of well documented and standardized information between organizations. This may help to explain why the contract manufacturing of printed circuit boards in the electronics industry has become such a big business. Printed circuit boards designs, can be fully specified in writing and transmitted electronically to suppliers. Modular product designs, in which the interfaces between different components and subsystems are well specified and standardized also enables coordination without vertical integration. Process development requires extensive coordination and communication between process R&D and manufacturing. Successfully transferring the process from the lab to the plant requires R&D personnel to go to the plant, often for an extended period of time, to set up the process and supervise initial test batches. If every plant that assembled similar products were allowed complete freedom in planning its production of various products, without considering the production and inventory decisions of other assembly plants, then the total network would either under-produce or over-produce. If stock-outs were costly then the firm might plan to produce more than the forecasted demand. If all plants accumulated buffer inventories, the total inventory costs across the entire network would be higher than desirable. Standardizing information systems, databases, part numbers, and other protocols also can help facilitate the exchange of necessary information. As a company's sales and product offerings increase, the resulting increase in complexity often causes the central organization to lose control over the activities of its facility network. When this is recognized usually in conjunction with some sort of crisis—the natural inclination is to centralize control and strengthen the central organization. Over time a series of such decisions inevitably reduces the authority of facility managers. The earlier problem was that these infrastructural decisions were the same for each plant, even though different plants-by design-had very different missions and production problems. A plant producing mostly low-volume products on manually operated equipment, would naturally experience higher set-up and inventory costs than a plant that produced mostly high-volume products on automated equipment. The product life cycle model provides a plausible logic that helps explain the patterns of innovation observed in many industries. It also brings critical competitive impact of the emergence of a dominant design and provides insight into why established firms in mature industries tend to experience difficulties adapting to radical product or process innovations. It focuses on cost reduction as the primary goal of process innovation. This implies that firms have an incentive to develop new processes only in the intermediate phases of an industry's life, after opportunities for new product innovation is depleted and production volumes are sufficiently high to justify specialized equipment. Organizational competencies required for product innovation are fundamentally different from-and in conflict with-the capabilities required for process innovation. Investment in specialized process technologies are often viewed as a potential hindrance to further product innovation, by causing firms to hesitate introducing new products that would make their existing process technologies obsolete. Yet there are businesses with strong product and process R&D capabilities that exist peacefully, and actually complement one another. In industries like pharmaceuticals, semiconductors, specialty chemicals and advanced materials, not only do product and process technologies evolved rapidly, they must be carefully synchronized. In some assembled products the connection between product and process might be tighter than the product lifecycle model. Producing miniaturized product designs for medical devices, instruments and consumer electronics often requires the development of processes having extremely high precision. Process development can be a bottleneck for product launch, particularly where process technologies are relatively complex and need to be customized to the design of a specific product. In order for process design to be successfully carried out in parallel with product design, a far more flexible process development capability is required. Fast process development can make it less imperative for an organization to adopt simultaneous engineering. The ability to carry out development sequentially, without extending the new product introduction date can reduce the financial risks associated with the development. The focus of prototyping, however is generated on identifying problems with product design. Prototyping often are built in specialized departments using methods, technology, and workers that are vastly differently from those that will ultimately be used when product will be introduced commercially. Very often process design problems, or problems with manufacturability of a design are not revealed until later stages of the development cycle, when formal pilot production runs are made. Depending on the product and the context, this may be too late and such problems may not be resolved by the time commercial production starts. One way to address this problem is to construct prototypes using a process that more closely resembles the operating environment in which commercial product will ultimately be produced, by taking the key elements of the final production environment to provide important feedback about manufacturing issues.

Operations tends to generate ideas for simplifying the design of the product or otherwise improving its production and delivery. R&D and engineering seek opportunities to exploit the latest technology and reduce costs for projects that might allow them to enter entirely new markets. Although top management is likely to be directly concerned with long range planning, operating level managers typically handle work order scheduling and dispatching. Annual capacity planning usually involves senior operations or facilities managers and their functional counterparts in marketing, engineering and product development. The organizational level and composition of the project team also influences the political process through which the projects approval is achieved and the degree to which various constituencies within the firm support its implementation. A project team that includes a wide range of perspectives and develops a rich set of alternatives when addressing a given situation is less likely to adopt a standard approach that overlooks important factors. Some companies assign two different teams to the same project, so as to introduce an element of competition into the development of innovative alternatives, and to provide an incentive to thoroughly investigate common ones. Another important factor is identifying the actions and resources that will have the greatest on the overall success of the project. Taking the example of an oilfield equipment manufacturer, this required identifying the major tasks required to support a sequence of capacity/facilities decisions over a five-year period, estimating the skills that would be required at each step along the way.

Considering a proposed investments option value, a pharmaceutical company that is confronted with three proposals, each of which would require a major investment. The first from the company's manufacturing organization, would enable the replacement and modernization of some existing equipment at one of its chemical plants. This will reduce the plant's operating costs and increase its capacity and flexibility. The second is use of internet for faster sharing of information. The third part is that the new chemical equipment essentially replicates existing operations and promises improved profitability in a well established business. The R&D investment in this can generate new scientific knowledge.

Organizations can study their performance and try to develop better ways to do their work. They usually have far more resources at their disposal. Organizations can hire and train process engineers and develop superior methods. They can replace resources that are expensive or in short supply with better alternatives-while individuals must live with their own physical and mental constraints. As organizations get larger they can create and exploit economies of scale, which can be obtained through a variety of management actions, including the use of higher volume facilities that require less labor and have lower capital cost per unit of capacity. This permits increased throughput without a proportional increase in people and capital, or reduced changeover costs if specific facilities are dedicated to certain high-volume products or services. Over an intermediate time frame, on the order of one to three years, an organization can recruit more effective people, put them to work identifying problems and proposing solutions, conducting process R&D, reorganizing work flows, and designing new products. Building and exploiting scale advantages, introducing a wholly different product or process technology, or redefining the game, which require several years of effort. Analog devices, which designs and manufactures specialized I.C.s came to the conclusion that the time required by an organization to achieve a given amount of improvement is largely a function of the elapsed time it takes to identify and eliminate problems. The spirit of TQM is much different, however, particularly in its emphasis of delegating primary responsibility to the people who work with a process, on improving existing processes rather than replacing them with entirely new processes on pursuing long-term goals through small steps rather than major leaps. Breakthrough improvements are likely to require major expenditures of funds and peoples time. A great deal of staff involvement is required, and the expertise of highly specialized people-financial analysts, strategic planners, legal experts, scientists, outside consultants or public relations personnel. Because of the magnitude of funds required to implement a strategic leap, the timing of such changes becomes important. On the other hand decline in profits, an increase in interest rates, an unexpectedly attractive alternative use of funds-all can delay a project. Those who succeed become heroes.

While the range of marketing options is limited by factory capabilities today, with the advent of technologies like CAD and CAM, continuous assembly line flows of dissimilar items will be possible through simple programming changes that will lead to greater production of customized products. Large buying firms are developing forecasting techniques to enable them to estimate time periods in which major technology developments might occur. Marketers must also monitor technological change if they hope to adopt marketing strategy with sufficient speed and accuracy to make the most of scientific breakthroughs. Product analysis consists of developing a list of criteria considered relevant to the needs of the target market, assigning weights to each of those criteria considered relevant to the needs of the target market, assigning weights of each of those criteria, and developing a rating scale to determine whether the product under consideration has a high or low probability of success in the marketplace. Lists of product criteria that specifically relate to functional areas of customer firms can also be developed. By questioning purchasing agents and other influencers within customer firms, weights can be assigned to the importance of criteria for various functional areas. Unlike the consumer market where products are normally marketed through one or two channels, most industrial marketers face diverse markets that must be reached through a multiplicity of channels-each requiring a different marketing approach. A producer of communications equipment, may market to such diverse segments as commercial, institutional, and governmental market, each of which requires a unique marketing plan. When marketing emphasizes tailor made products and fast deliveries, manufacturing must be prepared to follow through with product output. Planning in the industrial marketing arena requires a higher degree of integrated effort across functional areas and a closer relationship with overall corporate strategy than in the consumer market. Marketing's role in strategic planning should be one of analyzing and interpreting external, or market-related, information as well as internal or company-related information to spot opportunities and assess the company's strengths and weaknesses in respect to competing in the marketplace.

Product or market management systems concentrate on selling and improving products that concentrate on the desires of individual markets and may bring about the product or marketing changes that are beneficial to their markets, but not for the product in the majority of markets. As a product begins to enter the rapid growth stage, the emphasis of product strategy shifts to improving product design, improving distribution service, and lowering price as increasing product demand, accompanied by accumulated production experience. As market demand increases, product design and other aspects of the product offering must be changed to meet both low end and premium market segment needs. To manage the product line, industrial marketers can utilize product evaluation matrices and perceptual mapping to determine the most appropriate strategies for products and lines. Product matrices enable the marketer to track where a product is in its life cycle. Both matrix evaluation and perceptual mapping are useful in deciding whether to reposition or drop an existing product or to add a new product. Systems marketing is becoming an increasingly vital strategy for differentiating a firms product offering from competitors. Under the concept of systems marketing the firm offers more than a product; it offers customers a personalized service that is tailored to meet individual customer needs. While systems marketing requires greater responsibility to the customer, it provides additional benefits to both the firm and the customer. An average distributor lacks the technical competence therefore in case of specialized products customer engineering departments have a habit of redesigning special products from time to time, which can leave the distributor with a useless inventory of expensive parts that no one wants, including the manufacturer. It usually takes better control, communication and relationship to sell specialized products direct. Under the concept of systems marketing, the vendor produces and supplies all the major parts and services needed by customer firms. The results in increased revenues from tie-in sales of related products; reduced unit costs through common advertising, sales promotion, and increased productivity of the sales force and other channel members and brand loyalty. Customers experience reduced costs, in the development and procurement of a system, in sourcing suppliers and in reduction of inventory costs.

The importance of physical distribution and its impact on marketing objectives, depends on the type of product being marketed, the needs of the customer, and the structure of the distribution channel. Where products are used as inputs in the manufacture of other end products, buyers normally face a wide range of problems, including storage, stock control, order processing and traffic management. Thus, suppliers of component parts frequently face challenging logistical performance demands from their customers. Suppliers of heavy equipment, on the other hand, are more concerned with the problems of meeting scheduled delivery dates than with the maintenance of a finished goods inventory and, therefore, tend to have relatively low logistical service requirements. Logistical service levels affect the relationship between the manufacturer and customer as well as the operations of channel members. Inefficient service to middlemen either increases their costs, by forcing them to carry higher inventory level, or result in stock-outs, leading to a loss of business. A five percent reduction in service at this level can result in 20% decrease in sales to end markets. Both the length and consistency of the order cycle period affect the level of distributor inventories, which generally represent their highest asset investment and largest distribution expense. Public warehousing on the other hand can also be used to supplement or replace distributors in a market, as well as to support the sales force or manufacturers representatives. Inventories act as a buffer against supply and demand uncertainties as an economic trade-off to transportation, production and other conflicting costs. Production and demand are rarely in perfect balance. Operating deficiencies, such as delayed shipments or inconsistent carrier performance occur. Because of machine breakdowns or a sudden surge in market demand, industrial customers cannot always predict their requirements with certainty. The purpose behind training in industry and market trends is to develop salespeople who are knowledgeable about current business conditions within specific industries and markets of the vendor. Such knowledge enables salespeople, to understand modern trade practices, such as reduction in inventory levels in response to increased interest rates. Industrial salespeople use their experience with the buying firm, along with questioning and observing, to identify buying center members and predict influence and conflict resolution patterns. It may be understood in one firm, but may be different in similar firms, and they will tend to differ even more between firms in different industries.

    Catalogs also support the efforts of distributors because it is not always possible for them to carry in inventory all the items a manufacturer supplies. Most manufacturers provide their distributors with loose-leaf catalogs so that non-inventoried items can be located and ordered quickly from the catalog. Data sheets provide detailed technical information on such things as product dimensions, efficiencies, performance data, and cost savings, and thus are an important complement to the personal selling effort. Sales people seldom have all the answers that technical buyers require. When data sheets are prepared so that key selling points and technical information are presented in a clear, persuasive, credible manner, they can be powerful sales tools. Data sheets should include enough technical and product performance information to assist customers in their decision making and should be left by sales people with the appropriate decision makers. Marketing objectives indicate what is to be accomplished through advertising to achieve corporate objective. If the corporate objective is to increase return on stockholders equity by 5%, then the marketing objective would be increasing sales by 30%. To ensure that advertising objectives are being achieved and that money is being spent wisely, its effectiveness should be evaluated. Before it is implemented it can be measured by pretesting, its effectiveness can be measured by post-testing. Industrial advertising is used to reach unknown or inaccessible buying influence, to create awareness of the company, to enhance the sales call, to increase the overall effectiveness of the selling effort and to support distributors effort. While media usage generally differs from that used in the consumer market, the same principles apply in developing advertising and other promotional strategy. Further complicating the marketers task is the fact that pricing decisions must also consider cost, market demand, competition and government regulations. They also influence channel decisions and relationship because they affect the profit margins of distributors, the commissions of manufacturers representatives, and in turn the price to industrial end users and ultimate consumers. Penetration pricing is based on the assumption that demand for the product is highly elastic. By setting a relatively low price, the firm hopes to stimulate market growth and capture a large share of it. The advantage is that penetration pricing tends to discourage competition, because there is less opportunity to reap an unusually high return on investment. Penetration pricing may also be used to achieve economies of scale. Buyers are concerned with the evaluated price of a product, that is the total cost of owning and using the product. Such costs include in addition to the sellers price, transportation charges, the cost of installing capital equipment, inventory carrying costs for parts and material, possible obsolescence, order processing costs, and less apparent costs such as production interruption caused by product failure, late delivery or poor technical support. A firm may also choose to offer its products or services to a number of diverse segments whose needs, product usage, or market responses are appreciably different. Differentiated marketing strategy, to meet differences among target markets, increases overall costs to such areas as product development and modification, production, marketing and administration. In concentrated market selection even though a number of diverse segments exists whose needs could be satisfied through product and market variations when company resources are limited, the company may go with one of few markets and a strong market position can be achieved. In niche marketing which is another form industrial marketers are coming to realize that technical innovation, price, or direct selling are not enough to succeed in today's competitive marketplace which depends on trend or if the market can be divided into large enough niches.

Product value is related to the buyers sensitivity to price. Price sensitivity varies with purchasers, over time and from one set of circumstances to another. The buyer who can pass on the cost of a purchase is less likely to be price sensitive than one who cannot. Product price may be less important to engineers than performance variables, less important than reliable delivery to manufacturing personnel, and less important than supplier innovation. Thus marketing is the most important idea for which the other above chapters can be successful. There are many means of controlling this marketing function and bring this production focus to a success.

Reference

1) Elwood S. Buffa (1969), Modern production management. John Wiley & Sons ltd. 30-37, 138-158, 223-253, 298-371, 435-511, 616-627.
2) Donald Del Mar (1985), Operations and industrial management, designing and managing productivity. McGraw-Hill. 85, 103-108, 226, 227, 262-265, 340-353, 361-372, 380-391, 434-443, 506, 581-605, 626, 627, 633.
3) Jeffrey N. Lowenthal (1994), Reengineering the organization: A step by step approach to corporate revitalization. Tata McGraw-Hill. 18-41, 56-77, 99-124.
4) Kenneth B. Kahn (2001), New Product Planning. Sage Publications. 11-55, 60-113, 139-171.
5) Michael Grieves(2006), Product Lifecycle Management. Tata McGraw-Hill. 3-25, 32-55, 78-143.
6) Kevin N. Otto and Kristin L. Wood (2001), Product design: Techniques in reverse engineering and new product development. Pearson education. 12-94, 115-149, 193-253, 329-413, 551-615, 817-871.
7) Michael E. McGrath(2001), Product Strategy for high technology companies. McGraw-Hill. 9-40, 53-99, 135-205, 213-259, 273-333.
8) Gary P. Pisano and Robert H. Hayes(1999), Manufacturing Rennaisance. Harvard Business Review Book. 27-30, 37, 48-60, 64-76, 99-112, 117-130, 176-188, 259-272, 276-284, 300-310, 317-329.
9) Bill Scott(1994), Manufacturing Planning Systems. McGraw Hill. 7-31, 89-148.
10) Steven C. Wheelwright and Kim B. Clark (1992), Revolutionizing product development. The Free Press. 8, 14, 23-25, 118-121, 145-151, 168, 169, 223-226, 263.
11) William M. Lindsay and Joseph A. Petrick (1997), Total Quality and organization development. St. Lucie Press. 328-330.

12) John B. Bonny and Joseph P. Frien (1973), Handbook of construction management and organization. Van Nostrand Reinhold Company. 5-12, 13-17, 64-77, 117, 118, 159, 175-177, 202-203, 258-260, 270-274, 411-413, 435, 482-483, 559.
13) Martin K. Starr (1976), Production management: Systems and synthesis. Prentice Hall. 29, 45, 123, 173-179, 187, 205, 267, 289, 339.
14) James L. Riggs (1987), Production systems: Planning, analysis and control. John Wiley& Sons. 27, 83-91, 101-122, 181-193, 228-230, 355-377, 405-410, 491-531, 545-611.
15) Harry Cather, Roger Morris and Joe Wilkinson(2001), Business Skills for engineers and technologists. Butterworth-Heinemann. 148-187.
16) James Robert Taylor (1989), Quality control systems: Procedures for planning quality programs, McGraw-Hill. 46, 47, 110-112, 130-131, 166-170, 196, 200, 212, 279-281, 292-293, 370-372, 385, 386, 401-404.
17) A. V. Feigenbaum (1961), Total quality control, McGraw-Hill. 111-115, 330-332, 419-422, 440-444.
18) Richard G. Lamb (1995), Availability engineering and management for manufacturing plant performance, Prentice Hall International. 2-4, 9-11, 20-22, 25-27, 97-99, 121-123, 149-153, 178-180, 204, 212, 224-246, 236, 237, 238-239, 260-262, 276-278, 305-307, 321-323, 360, 361.
19) Greg Bounds, Lyle Yorks, Mel Adams, Gipsie Ramney (1994), Beyond Total quality management: Toward the emerging paradigm. McGraw-Hill. 78, 142-143, 175, 214, 215, 229, 245-247, 272-273, 278-280, 421, 660.
20) Dale H. Besterfield, Carol besterfield-Michna, Glen H. Besterfield, Mary Besterfield-Sacre (2003), Total Quality Management. Pearson education. 70, 130-134, 328, 376, 392.
21) Robert Hayes, Gary Pisano, David Upton, Steven Wheelwright (2005), Pursuing the competitive edge: Operations, strategy and technology. Wiley India. 47, 50, 67, 77, 89, 103, 126, 127, 159, 251, 270.
22) Robert R. Reeder, Edward G. Brierty and Betty H. Reeder (2003), Industrial marketing: Analysis, planning and control. Prentice-Hall U.S.A. 101, 138, 345, 449.

www.ingramcontent.com/pod-product-compliance
Lightning Source LLC
Chambersburg PA
CBHW030931180526
45163CB00002B/532